WHEE[...]

THE NO[...]

Christopher Moriarty

GILL AND MACMILLAN

First published 1980 by
Gill and Macmillan Ltd
15/17 Eden Quay
Dublin 1

with associated companies in
London, New York, Delhi, Hong Kong,
Johannesburg, Lagos, Melbourne,
Singapore, Tokyo

© Christopher Moriarty, 1980

7171 1032 X

TO MARY AND FERGUS

Cover photograph by Con Collins
Origination by Healyset, Dublin
Printed in Great Britain by Fletcher & Son Ltd, Norwich

CONTENTS

Introduction
1. Corrib Country: Galway to Oughterard
2. Eastern Connemara: Oughterard to Leenaun
3. Leenaun to Cleggan
4. Cleggan to Roundstone
5. Roundstone to Kilkieran
6. Kilkieran to Galway
7. Eastern Corrib: Galway to Headford
8. Headford to Cong
9. Cong to Westport
10. Westport to Louisburgh
11. Croagh Patrick: Louisburgh to Newport
12. Achill: Newport to Achill
13. The bogs of Bangor: Achill to Belmullet
14. North Mayo: Belmullet to Ballina
15. Lough Conn: Round trip from Ballina
16. Ballina to Sligo
17. Knocknarea: Round trip from Sligo
18. Lough Gill and Glencar: Round trip from Sligo
19. 'Under Ben Bulben': Sligo to Ballyshannon
20. Donegal town and Killybegs: Ballyshannon to Killybegs
21. Glencolumbkille: Round trip from Killybegs
22. Killybegs to Dunglow
23. Bloody Foreland: Dunglow to Dunfanaghy
24. Errigal: Round trip from Dunfanaghy
25. Sheep Haven and Lough Swilly: Dunfanaghy to Rathmullan
26. Lough Swilly: Rathmullan to Buncrana
27. Malin Head and Carndonagh: Buncrana to Carndonagh
28. Greencastle and the Grianan: Carndonagh to Letterkenny
29. Barnesmore and Lough Eske: Letterkenny to Donegal
30. Lough Derg and Lough Erne: Donegal to Manorhamilton
31. Lough Allen: Manorhamilton to Drumshanbo
32. Lough Meelagh and Lough Key: Drumshanbo to Boyle
33. Lough Arrow and Lough Gara: Round trip from Boyle
34. Rathcroghan: Boyle to Drumsna
35. Waterways: Drumsna to Roscommon
36. Lough Ree and Lough Funshinagh: Roscommon to Athlone
37. The Suck Valley: Athlone to Ballinasloe
38. Aughrim and Kilconnell: Ballinasloe to Loughrea
39. Athenry: Loughrea to Galway
40. Claregalway: Galway to Tuam
41. Knock and Kilmaine: Tuam to Ballinrobe
42. Lough Mask: Ballinrobe to Clonbur
43. Lough Corrib: Clonbur to Oughterard.

Recommended Reading
Index

INTRODUCTION

This book explores in the course of forty-three tours the region bounded to the south by a wavy line from Athlone to Galway, to the east by the Shannon and the Border, to north and to west by the broad Atlantic. It is a book for wanderers so it wanders a little outside its bounds, prompted to do so by occasional whims and by the more important principle that rules are made more interesting by the exceptions.

The second in a series of five, it was conceived as a guide for cyclists and therefore generally describes trips of less than 80km. The basic plan is to provide suggestions for touring for visitors with a week or two in which to travel. A second purpose is to introduce the country around a number of substantial towns to new residents. It is strictly a travelling book and does not aim to give a detailed picture of any of the towns on the journey. The tourist offices in all the larger towns have plenty of literature on that aspect. These offices also should be approached by anglers and others who need details on their specialities.

The book was planned by sitting down with the ordnance survey maps and summoning up memories of journeys made in the course of the past twenty-five years. This armchair study revealed places I had never seen and interesting routes unknown to me. So in 1979, I filled in many gaps in my own first-hand knowledge of the country. It was possible also to journey again over many of the roads I had visited in the past and, of course, to see on every one of them features which had escaped me.

The scenery in this north-western quarter of Ireland is rich. The land is poor. There was a time when the region was densely populated, but existence in those days was a bitter struggle whose rewards were little more than the ability to stay alive. Nowadays there are fewer people, but they are richer and healthier and a visitor may travel through less crowded but more prosperous land. The tourist of the twentieth century may rejoice in the solitude of the west and travel in peace in the knowledge that the country is no longer over-populated and that the majority of the residents are free from the past threats of poorhouse or emigration.

The routes begin in Galway, setting out to make a round trip of Connemara and the Mayo highlands as far north as Leenaun. It is an ancient region of acid rocks and poor land where most of the inhabitants live on the sea coast. From Galway again the road is northwards, but on the east side of the lakes through richer land where there is more in the way of antiquities and less of the rugged scenery.

Routes 10 to 16 run from Westport to Sligo, once again through poor but spectacular country, reaching by a causeway to Achill, the largest island off the coast and including much of Ireland's finest mountain and cliff scenery. Sligo lies in a fertile coastal strip, backed by the stupendous limestone mountains and faced with golden beaches. Antiquities, wild flowers and fishing abound from there to Donegal. Routes 20 to 24 cover north-western Donegal, back in the lonely scenery, while the next five keep mainly to the coast of eastern Donegal with some of the most ancient of early Christian remains.

The slightly unknown lands of Leitrim take the next three trips. Nature was perhaps a little less bounteous than usual, endowing the county with a waterlogged soil: too wet for any comfort in farming and yet not quite barren enough to make an excuse to give up altogether. Nonetheless the water does accumulate in places to make attractive lakes, and industrial archaeologists can rejoice in the abandoned ironworks.

Roscommon land is more fertile in places and borders a goodly expanse of the Shannon and its many lakes. Nobody knows how many the lakes are since the distinction between lake and river becomes excessively vague. It is lovely country with birds, boats and castles all the way to Athlone. The final seven journeys head back towards Galway, keeping mainly to the east, with its walled towns, abbeys and castles and the book ends with a couple of days back in the west again.

There is scope in that for five years of good summer holidays, just to allow a once-over trip. After that introduction you can settle somewhere and begin to explore in depths greater than this book can fathom. Places to stay appear with satisfactory frequency. The coastal parts have long abounded in all forms of accommodation. Inland regions have increasing numbers of guest-houses, especially where there are lakes and rivers nearby and a consequent population of angling visitors.

Single people or couples can usually find places to rest without advance booking but in the high season — July to August — larger parties would be wise to make reservations. Annual guides are issued to hotels, guest-houses, rented cottages and farmhouse accommodation.

Many sources of information, apart from my own impressions, have helped in preparing this book. A short reading list gives the titles of those which I have used most frequently. It is a particular pleasure to acknowledge Colette Copeland's inspiration and encouragement from start to finish.

1. CORRIB COUNTRY: GALWAY TO OUGHTERARD A fairly straight and very beautiful road leads directly to Oughterard. It begins by crossing the River Corrib by the Salmon Weir Bridge where you must stop to look at the salmon. When the water is low it flows gently and crystal clear over clean gravel. Beneath the flower beds on the right bank the salmon gather to wait until a flood comes. Then they head for the fish pass in the barrage and make their way through Lough Corrib to smaller rivers where they will breed in mid-winter. On the downstream side of the bridge eels are caught in autumn and kept in the large wooden cages. Further downstream lies the salmon trap. This may only be operated for four days every week and there is a 'Queen's Gap' which makes sure that some of the salmon can escape even during the four-day open season.

After the bridge you follow the main road to the right, passing the University whose main square was built of local limestone starting in 1846. The massive cathedral on the left was completed in 1965. About 3km of suburban and rapidly growing Galway leads at length to more open spaces and a view down on the right of Lough Corrib. A large white triangular pillar, looking rather like a yacht, marks the entrance to the navigation canal which bypasses many wanderings and shallows of the main river. From the hilltop the scenery to north and east is flat, based on Carboniferous limestone which has been dissolved away in places to form lake basins. To the west lie older rocks and hilly country: the lower hills are of Galway granite, much of it a beautiful pink stone, while the higher hills towards the north are older, Dalradian metamorphic rocks which include the beautiful green Connemara marble, obtainable cut and polished at all the best souvenir shops.

At Moycullen you can leave the main road for a longer route which runs close to the lake. Burnthouse is signposted as a right turn and the road leads down to a quay dating from the 1850s and the great days of the Corrib waterway. This is the narrowest part of the lake and marks a division between a shallow, weedy south basin and a very deep, island-studded north section.

The high point of the journey is Aughnanure Castle, requiring one more diversion from the main road, just before entering Oughterard. It was built by the O'Flaherty's early in the sixteenth century and in those days was well protected by water, most of which has since been diverted. It remains a magnificent building with formidable rocky surroundings and a six-storey keep, commanding the country for many miles around.

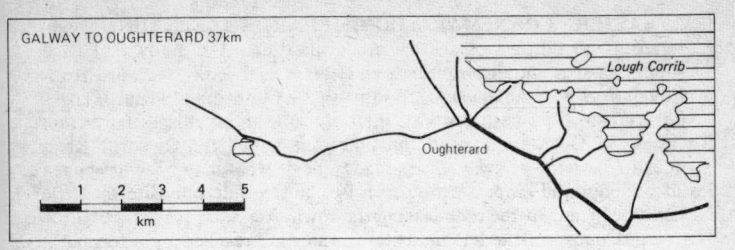

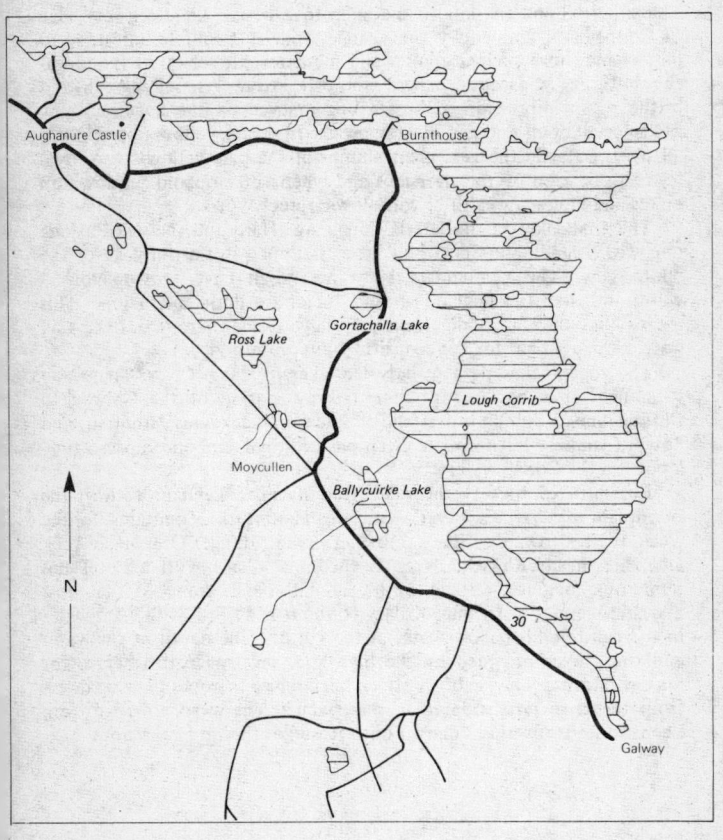

GALWAY TO OUGHTERARD 37km

2. EASTERN CONNEMARA: OUGHTERARD TO LEENAUN

Oughterard is an outpost of the eastern civilisation. It is a town of large shops, garages, hotels, churches and things and looks eastwards over Lough Corrib to the lowlands. To the west is Connemara, a land of lakes, bog and small homesteads with the only substantial villages far out on the coast. Oughterard stands on limestone which the Owenriff River does its best to eat away. The arched side of what may once have been an underground cavern can be seen by the riverside opposite the little park to the left of the road leaving the town.

A signpost to the left indicates a waterfall, reached by a footpath. The waterfall and the hill on the main road past it lie at the very edge of Connemara, defined by the change from soft soluble limestone to harder and more ancient granite and metamorphic rocks. At the top of the hill the landscape changes abruptly, from generally green and fertile to an impression of brown bog relieved on the lower hills by fields, small fields encaged by stone walls. In spring, yellow gorse blooms all over. Later in the year great clumps of the pale yellow-green royal fern can be seen by the riversides and when you stop and get down on hands and knees, a wealth of wild flowers greets you.

The first lake on the left is Lough Agraffard and the next, a long one with islands and Scots pine trees, is Lough Bofin, the lake of the white cow. The Connemara lakes nearly all have brown-coloured water and, like the bogland around them, are deficient in lime. This means that they are sadly lacking in large resident trout but the acid waters are just right for the beautiful white waterlily.

The road makes its way between lakes to Maam Cross. There you turn right, passing the one-time railway station of the Galway to Clifden line. You climb over the shoulder of Leckavrea Mountain and down a winding hill through sheep pasture to Maam, once upon a time a port on the Corrib waterway.

For most of its way the road from Maam to Leenaun follows the floodplain of Joyce's River, with the Maumturk Mountains to the west. It rises towards Killary, crossing rather younger Ordovician rock and then heads downwards to Leenaun, a village with a hotel and numerous lodgings, tucked in to the hillside in some of the most majestic scenery in Ireland. Killary Harbour is a fjord, with deep water in the centre and shallow water at the mouth. The depth of the water and the shelter provided by the high hills have made it a centre for mussel farming. The shellfish attach themselves to ropes hanging down from the large rafts moored in the channel. The westward road from Leenaun leads towards Killary Youth Hostel at the tip of the fjord.

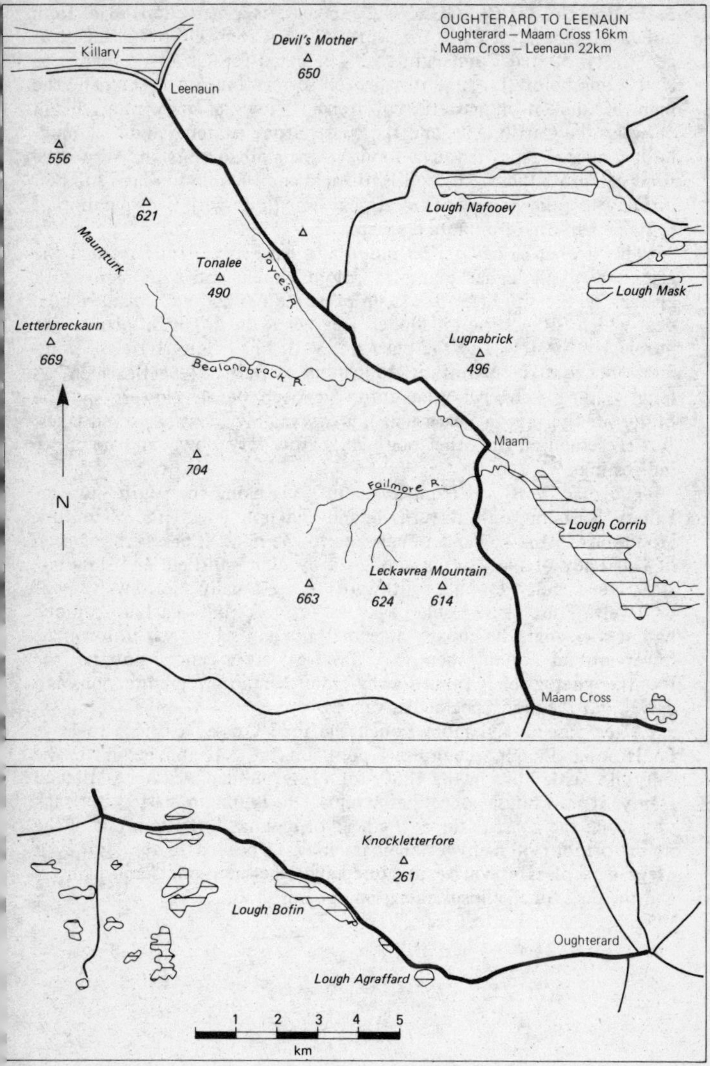
OUGHTERARD TO LEENAUN
Oughterard – Maam Cross 16km
Maam Cross – Leenaun 22km
Killary
Devil's Mother
650
Leenaun
556
621
Maumturk
Tonalee
490
Joyce's R.
Lough Nafooey
Lough Mask
Letterbreckaun
669
Bealanabrack R.
Lugnabrick
496
N
Maam
704
Failmore R.
Lough Corrib
Leckavrea Mountain
663
624
614
Maam Cross
Knockletterfore
261
Lough Bofin
Oughterard
Lough Agraffard
1
2
3
4
5
km

3. LEENAUN TO CLEGGAN Connemara is a marvellous place for a holiday, but a grim place for work. Oliver Cromwell in a moment of generosity offered Connaught to his defeated foes as an alternative to Hell. Long before his time it had been seen as a region to shun and the map of ancient monasteries of Ireland shows a conspicuous blank between the Corrib lakes and the coast. Stone churches and even mud-built monastic cities required food for their inhabitants and very little food can grow there. The soil is too acid and the rain too heavy to permit anything in the way of traditional agriculture with the exception of raising a handful of mountain sheep.

The steeper slopes of the mountains have successfully resisted the attempts of all higher plants to colonise them and bare, shiny rock glistens in the sun. The less steep parts are clothed with blanket bog, peat which follows the hill slopes. Heather is the dominant plant; deep purple bell heather and the paler ling with small flowers are the common ones, but there are rarities including St Dabeoc's heath which has long, trailing stems with beautiful big deep purple flowers and the bushy Mediterranean heath which grows mainly by streams and lakes. But these and all the other bog plants grow very slowly and are pretty indigestible.

The road westward from Leenaun leads along the south shore of Killary Harbour until it turns inland and uphill with the Maumturk Mountains to the left and Lough Fee to the right. It passes the Church of Our Lady of the Wayside, designed by Leo Mansfield and standing, stark and angular, looking southwards to the equally stark Twelve Bens or Twelve Pins. These noble peaks are formed from quartzite, a much harder rock than the equally ancient Dalradian schists which form the lower ground around them. The Twelve were a central point in the Ice Age when glaciers flowed away from them in several directions and carved out the more spectacular valleys.

After passing Kylemore Lough the road crosses a bridge to leave Poulacappal Lough, the horse's pool, on the left and behind it the fairytale castle built in the 1860s for a Liverpudlian merchant, Mitchell Henry. It now houses Bénédictine nuns. One kilometre past Letterfrack you reach the coast again, at the head of Ballinakill Harbour one of the more tortuous of many Connemara inlets. The end of the journey is Cleggan, a pleasant village inhabited by fishermen, poets and painters and the port for the hospitable island of Inishbofin.

LEENAUN TO CLEGGAN 32km

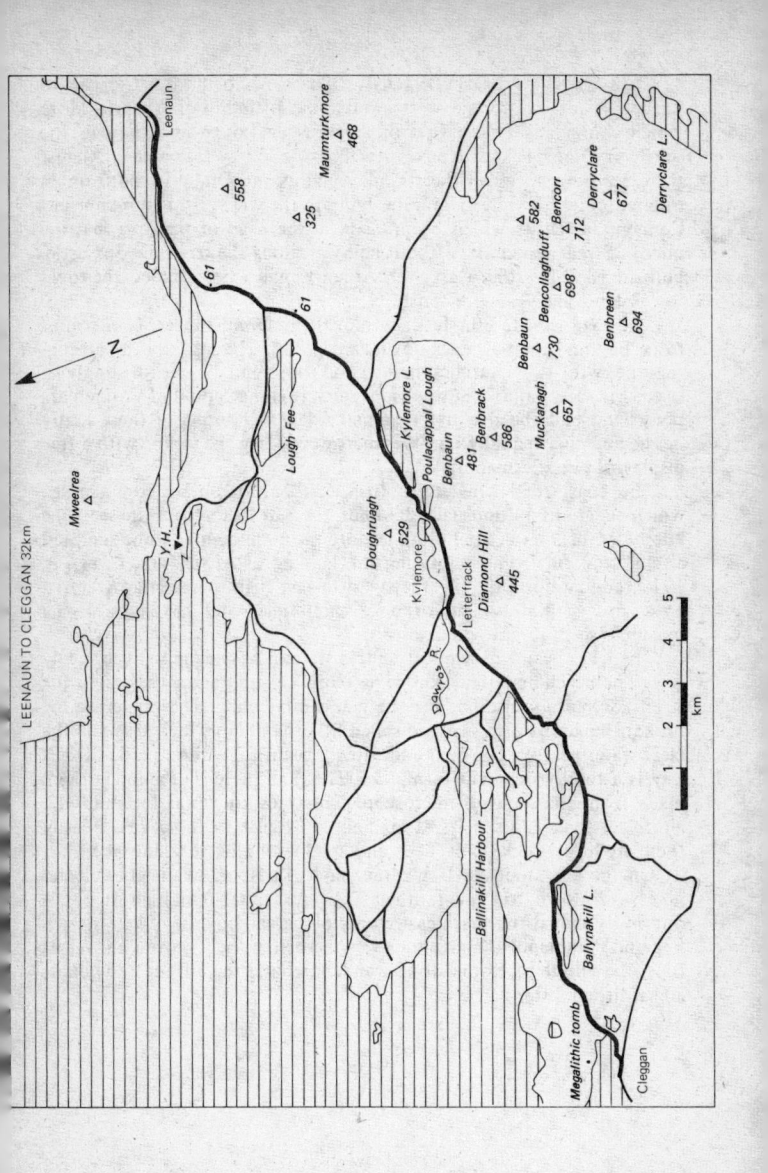

4. CLEGGAN TO ROUNDSTONE The slow road from Cleggan to Clifden heads out to the west around the little hill of Aughrus More which commands a view first of Aughrusbeg Lough and then to the south of Omey Island. You can walk to it at low tide and in August there are pony races on the strand. Aughrus and Omey Island form an isolated patch of Galway granite, lying to the west of the more ancient Connemara schists which begin again at the head of the long, narrow inlet of Streamstown Bay. About half way along the bay is Doon Castle, built in 1815 by John Darcy, an Athenry man who founded the town of Clifden three years previously.

The road rises to 60m just south of the innermost recess of Streamstown Bay and then zig-zags downwards again. The village is a substantial one, with two churches, many good shops and a plentiful supply of tweed, sweaters and less useful souvenirs. It is the capital of Connemara pony land and the site of the annual August gathering of these hardy beasts and their equally hardy owners, rewarding the visitor with a fine display of ponyflesh and tweed.

The coast road runs south from Clifden, crossing a stone bridge which separates an unusual tidal inlet, the Salt Lake, from the sea. One kilometre further on, a right turn leads to the monument, a stone-sculpted aircraft tail fin, commemorating the landing of Alcock and Brown in 1919, ending abruptly the first west-to-east flight across the Atlantic. Even today, in this land of bog, small fields and haycocks, flying machines seem to have no place.

There are beautiful white strands in Mannin Bay and in Ballyconneely Bay. The beach material is known as 'coral'. It isn't actually coral in the strict zoological sense but is nonetheless interesting. The grains are the broken skeletons of a seaweed called lithothamnion which grows in the clear water nearby. The next and equally beautiful white strand of Dog's Bay is a totally different formation. The sand there is of animal origin, made from the shells of microscopic creatures known as foraminifera. No fewer than 124 species of animals contribute to the beach. Nearby there are lovely rock pools, deep and lined with pink coralline weed.

On the left, opposite Dog's Bay stands Errisbeg, an ancient volcano now worn down to a saw-toothed stump just over 300m high. It stands out on its own at the south-east corner of a great expanse of lake-strewn bog and commands a marvellous view across to the Twelve Pins. At its foot, the village of Roundstone wanders around the hillside and guards a neat little lobster harbour.

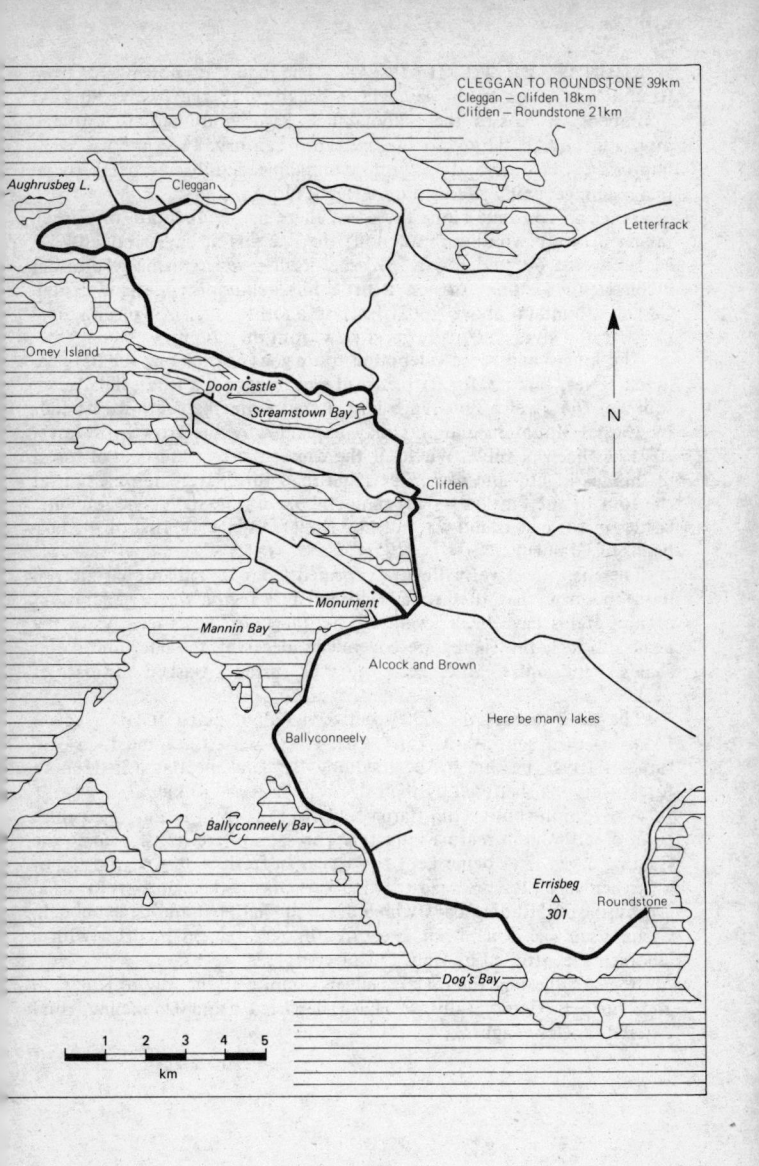

CLEGGAN TO ROUNDSTONE 39km
Cleggan – Clifden 18km
Clifden – Roundstone 21km

Aughrusbeg L.
Cleggan
Letterfrack
Omey Island
Doon Castle
Streamstown Bay
N
Clifden
Monument
Mannin Bay
Alcock and Brown
Here be many lakes
Ballyconneely
Ballyconneely Bay
Errisbeg
△
301
Roundstone
Dog's Bay

1 2 3 4 5
km

13

5. ROUNDSTONE TO KILKIERAN The road leads northwards from Roundstone, close to the sea, with a backdrop of the Twelve Pins. At Toombeola it crosses the Ballynahinch River and there is a ruined monastic church dating to the sixteenth century. It is not the most impressive of ruins and is more remarkable simply for being there, in a region generally shunned by affluent monks.

You can continue along the coast there in the direction of Cashel, taking a lovely winding route along the margins of bays studded with islets covered by golden wrack. Cashel itself owes its name to a rather inconspicuous stone fort on a little hill behind the Zetland Hotel. Cashel Mountain above the village is another ancient volcano, like Errisbeg and gives an equally good view from the summit.

The longer and more celebrated route goes north along the Ballynahinch River, famous for its plentiful and hungry sea trout. The valley south of the Twelve Pins range is sheltered from the south-west winds by Cashel Mountain and this may explain why the growth of forest trees has been possible. Whatever the cause, there is an island of forest in this sea of bog and rock. The main road turning to the east runs at the foot of the Pins with Ballynahinch Lake on the right. The romantic castle on the lake island was built by Donal O'Flaherty, first of the husbands of Granuaile.

The majestic Twelve Pins are formed from Dalradian quartzite, so hard and firm that they remain upright in a region where generations of mountains have been levelled. The quartzite shows clearly on the peaks, though the flanks are covered in places by the later and softer shales. Wind and weather keep the rock surfaces washed and bare of peat.

The road crosses the valley between Ballynahinch and Derryclare Lakes to turn southwards for Carna. It crosses a ridge and then continues flattish, passing by Bertraghboy Bay and meeting a little more forest, this one sheltered by the ridge of hills above Kilkieran.

A diversion south from Carna leads to Mweenish Island, the centre for a caged salmon rearing industry. The salmon are transferred to the floating cages after being kept for a year in fresh water. At the end of a further year they are ready for market. One of the major problems in the business is finding bays which are well sheltered and deep enough. Carna itself has long been a centre for research on shellfish with a laboratory controlled by Galway University.

Beneath the bog the rock is Galway Granite all the way to Kilkieran and further. Geologically we have departed from Connemara and entered Iar-Connaught.

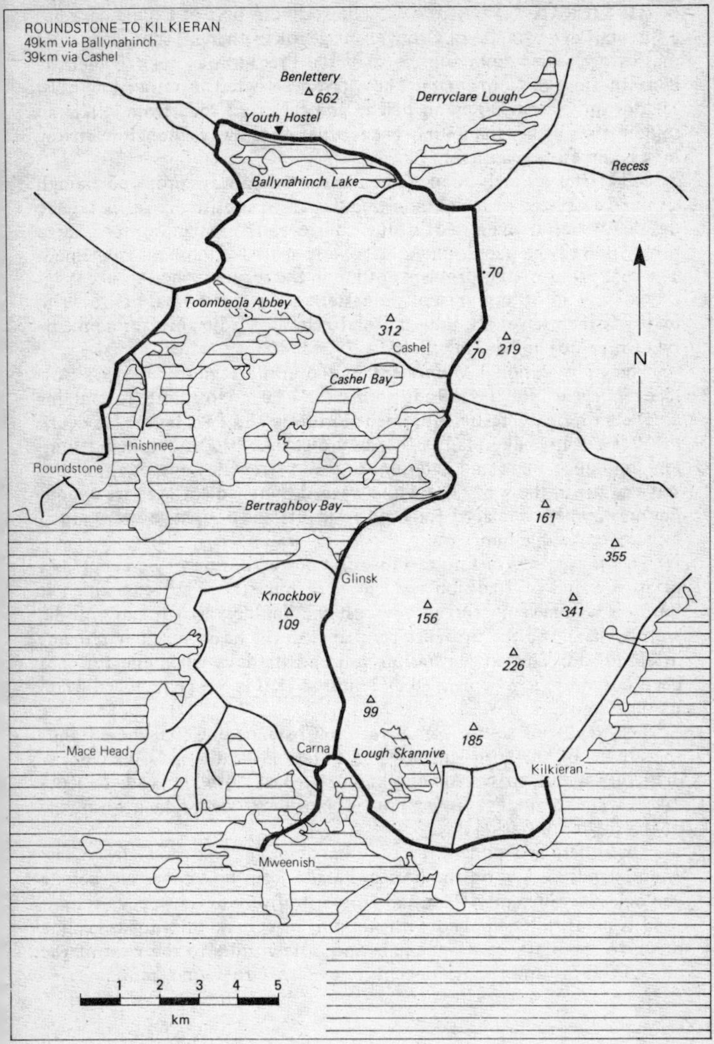
ROUNDSTONE TO KILKIERAN
49km via Ballynahinch
39km via Cashel
Benlettery
662
Derryclare Lough
Youth Hostel
Ballynahinch Lake
Recess
70
Toombeola Abbey
312
Cashel
70
219
N
Cashel Bay
Inishnee
Roundstone
Bertraghboy Bay
161
355
Glinsk
Knockboy
109
156
341
226
99
185
Mace Head
Carna
Lough Skannive
Kilkieran
Mweenish
1
2
3
4
5
km

6. KILKIERAN TO GALWAY

The southern part of Connemara has a foundation of granite of Ordovician age, older than most of the granite masses of Ireland but younger than the Precambrian rocks which lie beneath most of Connemara. They have weathered to rather low hills, seldom more than 300m in height and the coast road from Kilkieran seldom rises higher than 30m. The journey to Galway, though relatively long is therefore reasonably flat.

It is never a lonely road, since the seashore always provided enough fish and fertilizer to maintain a population of subsistence farmers. The desire for better living led in due course to the emigration of a large proportion of the people and a little more space for those that remained. The real proof of the problems of life in the region is the absence from the coast road of any ancient monasteries, castles or great houses. The by-roads themselves are unusual for Ireland in leading just for a mile or two to the bog and ending there.

The only National Monument in the entire region is Pearse's Cottage, snuggled into the hillside across the lake at Gortmore. It contains a collection of domestic equipment in use in the days before his death in 1916. Pearse, like many other city dwellers, had established a summer residence there and catering for visitors remains one of the mainstays of life in the west. The white-washed thatched cottages are dwindling in numbers, replaced for both residents and tourists by very much more comfortable bungalows.

To the east of Gortmore stands the power station of Screeb. It is a pleasing blend of tradition with modern industry. The peat which it burns is so unevenly spread amongst the boulders that it can only be won by hand. So the turf-cutter rather than the heavy machine remains in command. The power station will end its days when the turf has been cut away. It was planned and built so that it can be removed when its time comes.

The road runs south from Screeb to Costelloe or Casla where stands the studio of the Irish language radio station, Radio na Gaeltachta. A right turn at the crossroads one kilometre past Costelloe leads to Rossaveel where a modern fishing port is being developed, taking advantage of the shelter of Cashla Bay.

Then there is a straight run of 30km along the coast to Galway. The Aran Islands lie low on the horizon. Made from limestone they belong geologically to County Clare but administratively to Galway. The coast road is plentifully supplied with stopping places and little roads leading down to the seashore. Connemara ends a few miles to the west of the city of Galway and twentieth-century existence rules once more.

KILKIERAN TO GALWAY 66km

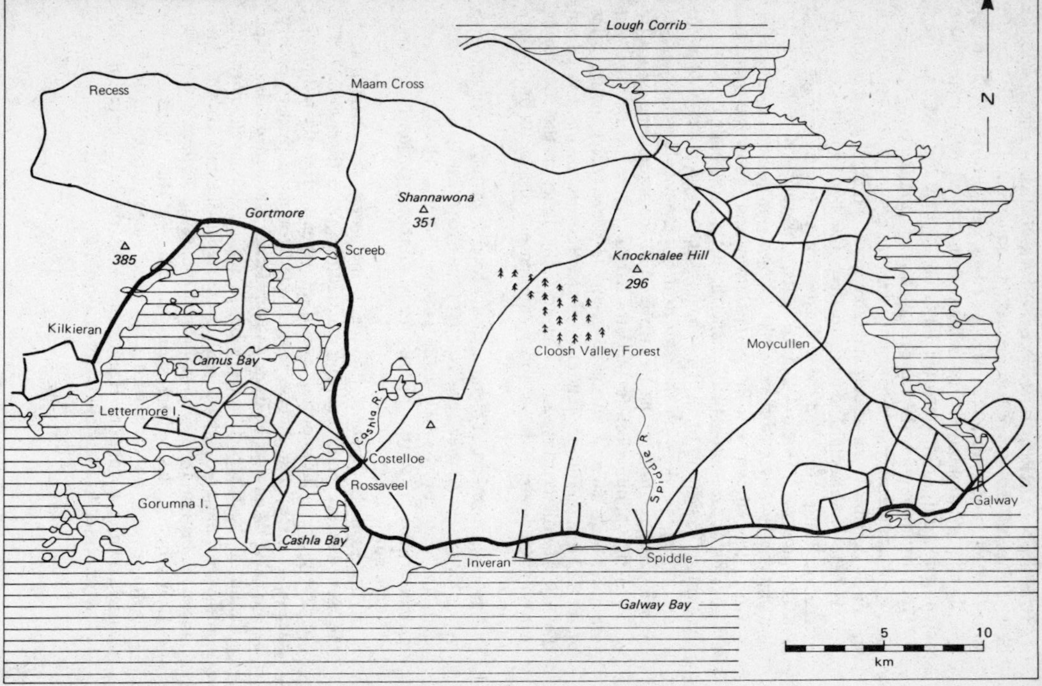

7. EASTERN CORRIB: GALWAY TO HEADFORD

The land to the east of Lough Corrib is a world apart from Connemara. The rock beneath it is Carboniferous limestone, weathered to a level plain by the River Corrib and its tributaries. The solid rock is coated by glacial gravel, composed mainly of fragmented limestone. Where the lake and rivers are kept within bounds the land is well drained and the general impression is of lush greenery, where Connemara was brown. There are salmon in Lough Corrib as well as eels and large trout. All in all it is a rich area and therefore well supplied with castles, churches and ancient farmsteads, marked as 'forts' on the Ordnance Survey maps. Drainage operations, in progress for nearly twenty years, seek to increase the area of dry land and have created the spoil heaps by the major rivers.

Go to the Salmon Weir Bridge in Galway and follow the river bank northwards as far as possible, passing the little stone-built dock where present-day navigation of the lakes begins. In the past it was possible to reach the sea by a lock on the right bank but the canal has been closed by a low bridge. Follow the Headford Road for about one kilometre north of the shopping centre and turn left at the crossroads for a visit to a quiet little harbour on the river, an old beech forest and the ruins of the noble mansion of Menlough Castle. Built by the Blake family in the seventeenth century and enlarged many times in the succeeding two hundred years, it has stood a ruin since a disastrous fire in July 1910.

The main road east of Menlough runs level and straight, crossing two rivers, the Clare and the Cregg. North of the Cregg turn left at the crossroads to head for the lake shore at Annaghdown. The lake changes character there from the shallow, reedy southern portion to the deep and dark north basin.

St Brendan the Navigator founded a monastery at Annaghdown in the sixth century and, according to tradition, died there in 577. The monastery grew in importance and 600 years after its foundation became the see of a diocese which lasted for more than a century, before being taken over by its neighbour, Tuam. The cathedral is a simple building of the fifteenth century but it includes a marvellous twelfth-century romanesque window with some delightful animals, the finest a big-eyed, big-mouthed beast munching some stone foliage.

Down by the lake shore stand the ruins of the priory, another fifteenth-century building with early work incorporated in it. From Annaghdown, the road to Headford follows the lake shore for 2km before returning to the main highway.

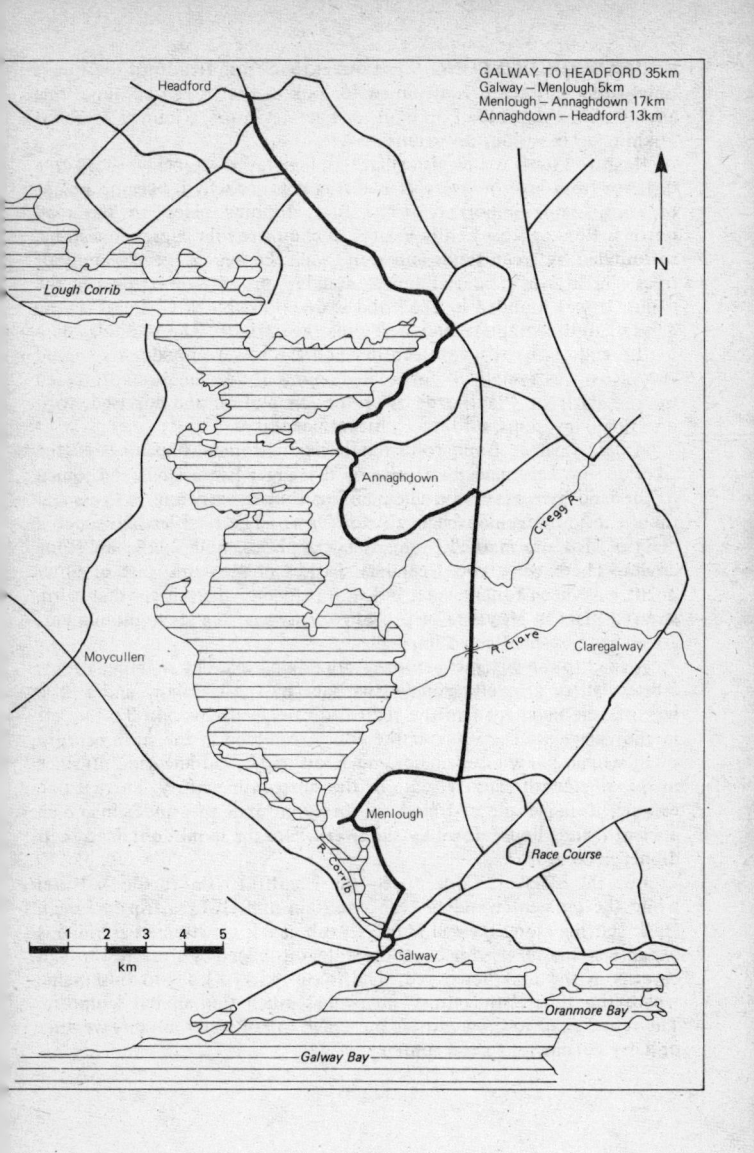

GALWAY TO HEADFORD 35km
Galway – Menlough 5km
Menlough – Annaghdown 17km
Annaghdown – Headford 13km

8. HEADFORD TO CONG

The direct road from Headford to Cong is only 18km but there is so much to look at that it can be quite long enough for a day-trip. For more energetic visitors a jouney of about 50km takes in various diversions.

Headford itself is a biggish village, though rather strangely placed at a distance from lake or rivers. It is difficult to see why it became a place of considerable importance. The first stopping place on the road north is Ross or Ross Errilly Friary, an exquisite ruin in grey limestone, surrounded by green fields and stone walls. Perhaps it is the scarcity of trees which gives it special appeal, standing proudly on its own in the plains. It was founded in 1357 and is described by H. G. Leask as the 'largest, most complete and best preserved friary'. The buildings date to the end of the fifteenth century and the tower provides a splendid view. Ross was a relatively fortunate community, having been protected by the Earls of Clanricarde after the Dissolution and survived, with occasional invasions, into the eighteenth century.

A left turn at Bunnafollistran leads by tortuous turnings to the lakeside and Inishmacatreer, one of the larger lake islands and joined to the land by a causeway. The main road turns westwards in Cross and there the journey may begin to slow down. The road leads through a plain of Moytura marked by many burial places, stone cairns and stone circles. There were two legendary battles of Moytura: one or other might have been fought here, but unfortunately there is another cairn-strewed plain in Moytirra of Co. Sligo. Anyway, the Mayo monuments are ancient, authentic and imposing.

A road to the left, just before entering Cong, leads by an impenetrable estate wall to a lovely secluded harbour by the lakeshore and a little way off the main road to the right is a cave in the woods. To the left in the village are the ruins of the abbey, founded in the sixth century by St Fechin but whose remains, much restored by Guinness munificence in the nineteenth century, date to the thirteenth century. There is fine carving, Romanesque and modern, lovely grounds to wander in and an ancient fishing house down by the river where the monks obtained their dinner in comfort.

For the affluent, Cong boasts the beautiful Ashford Castle Hotel while the indigent wanderer can entertain himself by a trip to Lough Mask starting along the sad Mask-Corrib canal, constructed at hideous expense and never used because the water disobliged by escaping through caverns in the rock-hewn bed. The route marked leads to Inishmaine where the thirteenth-century abbey has much fine animal sculpture. The return road to Cong crosses the canal, full of water in rainy weather or a dry cutting in a good summer.

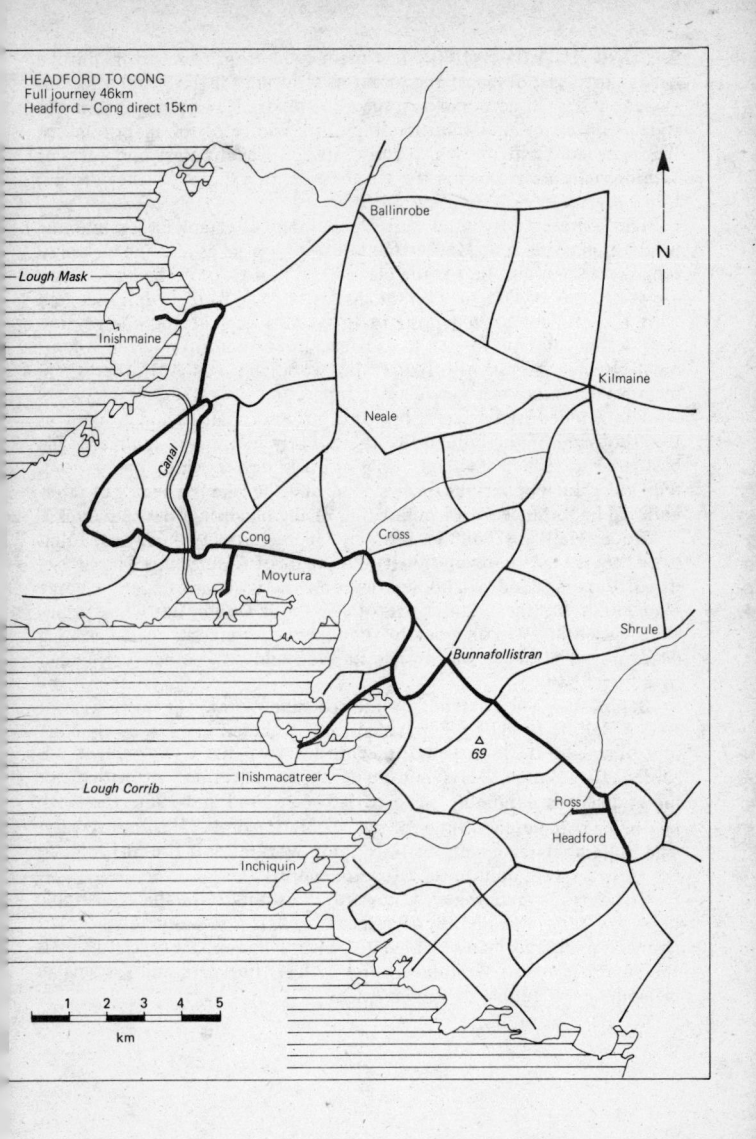

HEADFORD TO CONG
Full journey 46km
Headford – Cong direct 15km

9. CONG TO WESTPORT The main road from Cong to Ballinrobe heads north-east amongst the tombs of Moytura for the Neale where an ancient pillar stone stands at the crossroads. Having negotiated the traffic congestion of Ballinrobe, there is a choice of the main road for Westport and Castlebar which runs between Loughs Mask and Carra or turning right after crossing the River Robe for a longer journey around Lough Carra.

The more easterly road passes a number of estates before coming to a stopping place at Moore Hall, close to the lakeshore. The lake is a remarkable one and breeds the biggest and best trout in the land. There are great beds of lake rush on the margin and the lake bottom is coated with a cream-coloured deposit of lime. This deposit and the crystal-clear water combine to give the surface an extraordinary green colour. Small islands are plentiful and the woodland which clothes them includes the rather rare native aspen tree.

The wooded islands are a breeding place for mallard and as many as two thousand of these duck live there. Early morning in summer is the best time to visit to see the flotillas of ducklings. In winter many hundreds more duck of various species come and the lake is a centre of international importance for its population of the handsome shoveler duck.

Moore Hall was built in 1795 by George Moore whose son, John, ruled briefly as the revolutionary President of Connaught. The house, its surroundings and neighbours figure in the writings of a later George who left it for the brighter life of Paris and Dublin but whose ashes were buried in 1933 on a nearby island, the spot marked by a charming headstone. The house was burned in 1923 and now stands surrounded by a forest park.

Ballintober Abbey stands by the roadside 4km to the north-west of Moore Hall. It has had a happier history: founded in 1216 by the king of Connaught it flourished for centuries until the Cromwellians unroofed the church. Mass continued to be celebrated notwithstanding and it was admirably restored between 1963 and 1966, the work just being completed in time for the celebration of its 750th anniversary. The building dates mainly to restoration work after a fire in 1265 and the cloisters were built in the fifteenth century.

The road wanders gently towards Westport, attaining the noble height of 60m at Killavally. Westport itself is a pleasant town with a riverside mall, and many eighteenth-century houses. Its special pride is the superb classical Westport House with its fine park and gardens all welcoming the public for a modest fee.

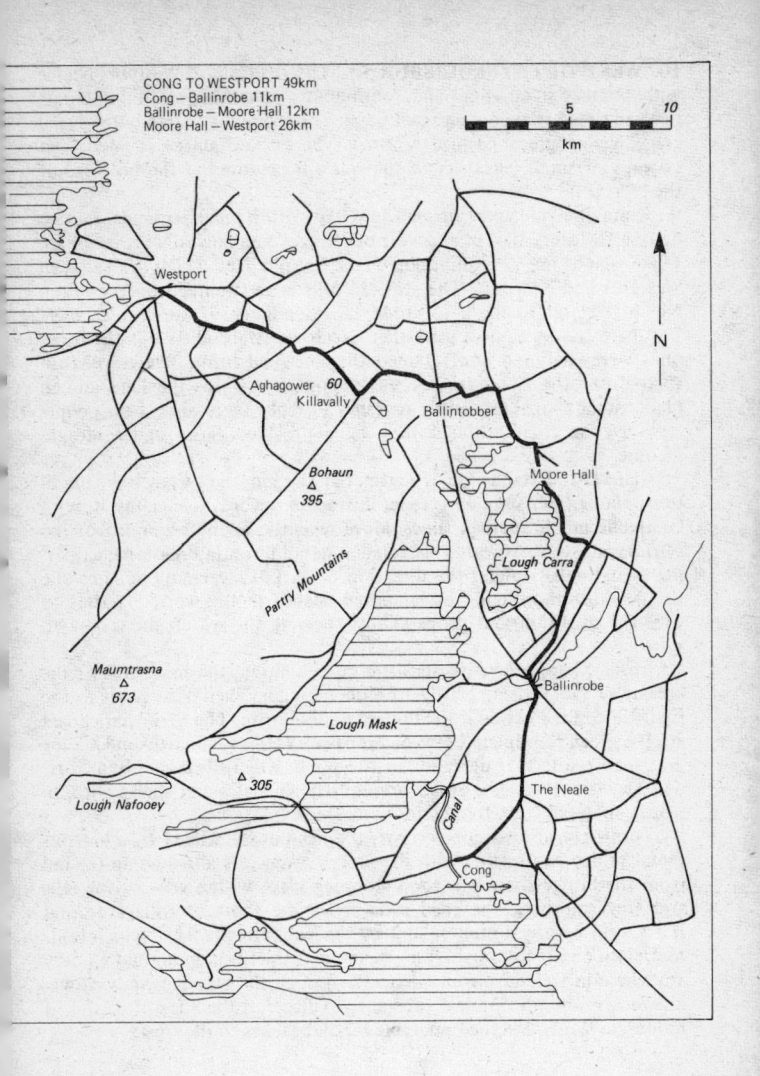

CONG TO WESTPORT 49km
Cong — Ballinrobe 11km
Ballinrobe — Moore Hall 12km
Moore Hall — Westport 26km

10. WESTPORT TO LOUISBURGH The road out of Westport begins with a rather steep climb and continues as something of an uphill past the little reed-fringed Creggan Lough. The ground is coated with glacial gravel giving green pasture or gorse where the drainage is good, and swamps or small lakes where the water is captured at the bottoms of the hills.

From the hill you can see Clew Bay with its many islands, said to be one for every day of the year but in fact totalling only eighty or so. These islands are a continuation of the drumlin land which lies between Westport and Newport. The seaward hills were swamped by the ocean which then set to work to erode the islands which stood in its way. This gave the outermost ones their steep westward cliffs but the inner ones were sheltered and retained their original form. The gravel torn away from the outer islands was deposited towards the land and in places joined smaller islands together to make large ones. Few people now live on them, though they once provided farms and a meagre income.

Clare Island stands like a sentinel at the mouth of Clew Bay. Tradition, though possibly not strict historical record, associates it with Granuaile in Elizabethan times. More recently, at the beginning of the century, it was surveyed in spectacular detail by an international gathering of naturalists under the direction of R. L. Praeger and remains one of the most thoroughly documented islands in the world. It rises to a height of 463m and drops almost sheer to the sea on the westward side.

From Knappagh, with its little stone church, the road follows the Owenwee valley rising gently to Moher Lough. Then it descends to the Erriff and stays beside it for the next 10km or so. The Erriff has carved itself a green floodplain between the Sheefry Hills to the right and Maumtrasna to the left. It descends to the sea in Killary between Ben Gorm and Devilsmother. The rocks are Ordovician slates and shales with, in places, material from tremendous volcanic explosions.

Turn right at Leenaun to cross the head of the Killary by a hideous metal bridge contrasting with the superb Aasleagh Falls. Just up the hill from the bridge there is a good stopping place with a view of the falls and Devilsmother. The road runs above the shore of Killary around Ben Gorm before turning inland by the Bundorragha River which leads to Delphi and Doo Lough, lying in some of the finest mountain scenery anywhere in Ireland. From Glencullin Lough the way is mainly downhill to Louisburgh, the last substantial village on the edge of a land of mountain slopes and incomparable sandy beaches to the west.

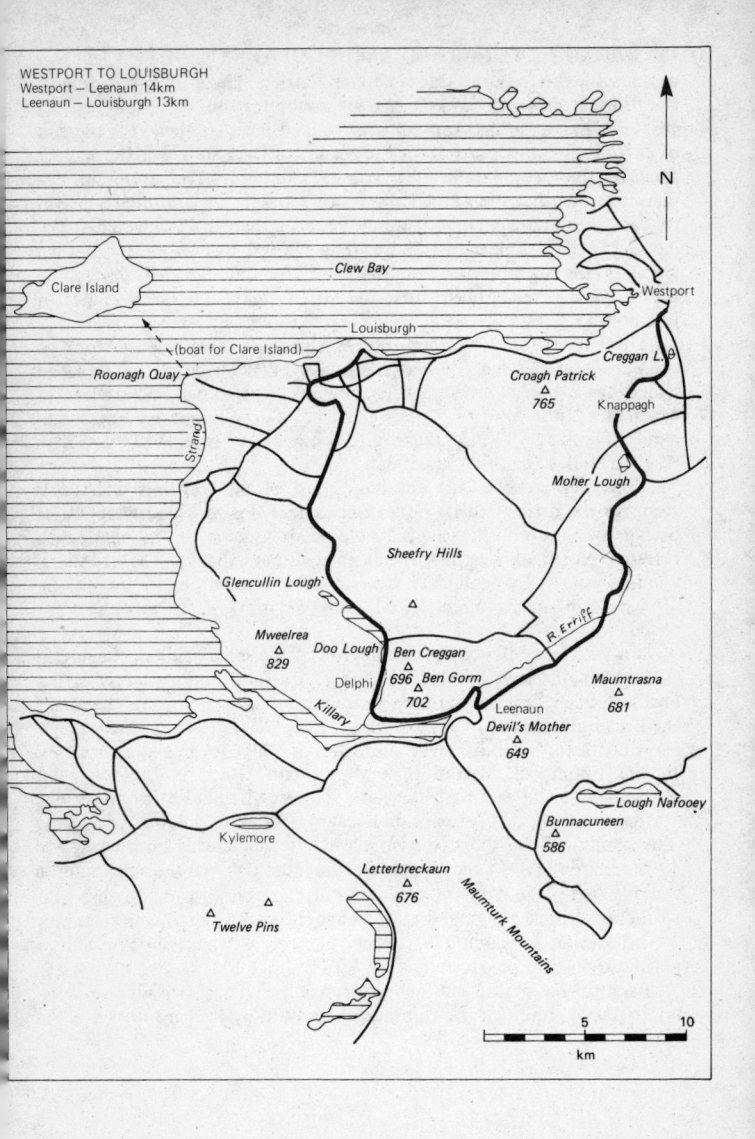

WESTPORT TO LOUISBURGH
Westport – Leenaun 14km
Leenaun – Louisburgh 13km

11. CROAGH PATRICK: LOUISBURGH TO NEWPORT Clew Bay is ruled by the holy mountain Croagh Patrick. The saint, according to tradition, spent forty days of extreme discomfort on its summit and for centuries past pilgrims from all over Ireland have climbed it at the end of July. Full compensation for the rigours of the climb over the scree is given by the incomparable view over hill and ocean. The mountain, like many of the other spectacular cones in Ireland, is made of quartzite but its date is Silurian, making it much younger than the Twelve Pins. The ice sheet which deposited the drumlins of Clew Bay and ground down much of the surroundings left the peak of Croagh Patrick exposed to the weather. The action of frost and sun shattered the rock and wore it to a point.

The road from Louisburgh to Westport passes along the foot of the mountain, though you may first make a little diversion to Old Head which has a pocket of ancient oak wood on its slopes and a pleasant beach at its foot. Murrisk is the starting point for pilgrimage or unaccompanied climb and is also the site of a monastery founded in 1457 by Hugh O'Malley for the Augustinians.

You keep close to the coast for most of the way into Westport, going to the quay with its rather imposing waterfront and warehouses dating to an overenthusiastic development scheme of the eighteenth century. North of Westport the main road goes through the drumlins, winding gently to avoid the steeper hills. The drumlins are oblong hills, pointing in the direction taken by the moving ice sheet and composed entirely of stones and gravel.

Newport straddles the beautiful river of the same name at the northeast corner of Clew Bay. Its main hotel is a fine georgian house with a lovely staircase and the Catholic church has an outstanding east window, the Last Judgement by Harry Clarke.

A northward turn off the road to Achill leads into an exquisite valley in the Nephinbeg Mountains between Ben Gorm to the west and Buckoogh to the east with the dark waters of Lough Feeagh in its bed. Furnace Lough, downstream of Feeagh, is tidal, an inlet of Clew Bay. The salmon of the short Burrishoole River which leads from Feeagh to Furnace are the most thoroughly documented fish. All the adult salmon which pass up the river to spawn and all the young going downstream to the sea are caught, measured and tagged at the experimental station of the Salmon Research Trust where pioneering experiments in salmon rearing are also in progress.

Back on the main road a short diversion to the west leads to Burrishoole Abbey, built for the Dominicans in 1486 by Richard Burke.

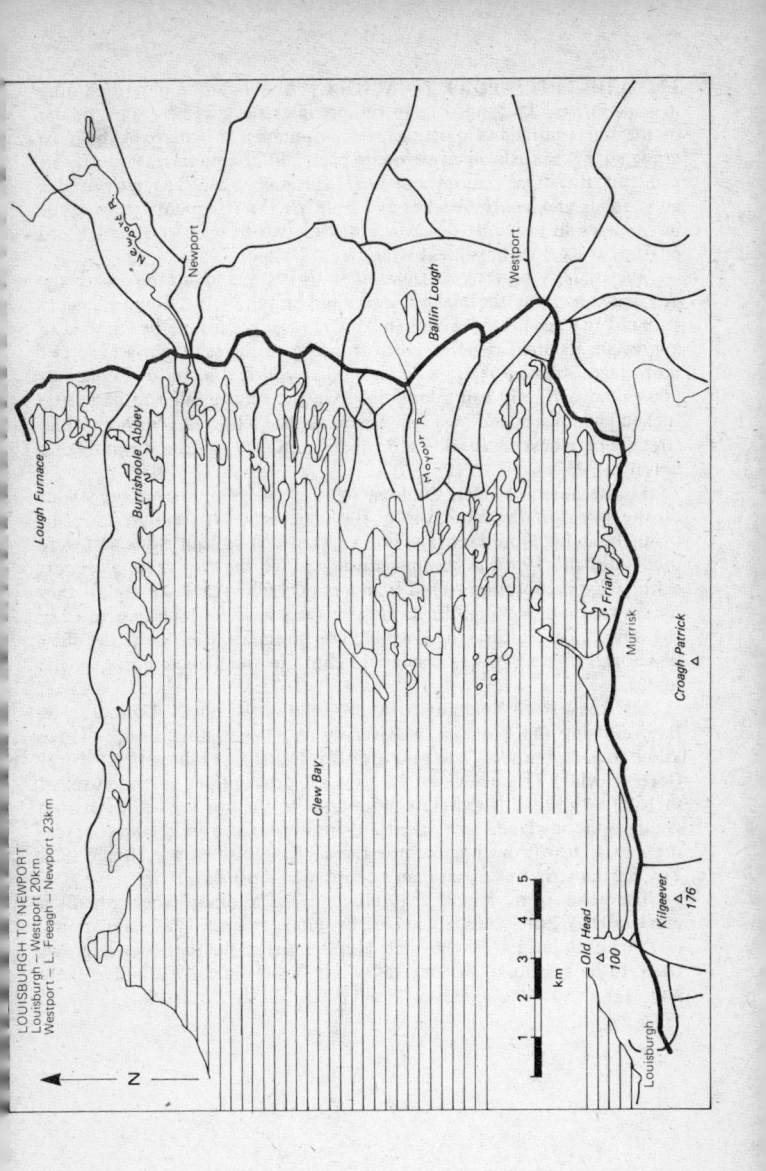

LOUISBURGH TO NEWPORT
Louisburgh – Westport 20km
Westport – L. Feeagh – Newport 23km

12. ACHILL: NEWPORT TO ACHILL

Achill can be described only in superlatives. It stands out in the ocean as the biggest island, holder of the finest cliffs and most shapely mountains. It is perhaps the most crowded by tourists in some of its parts but compensates by offering some of the most remote and beautiful landscapes. The crowds like good roads and sandy beaches and both are there in plenty, leaving the high slopes in peace. It deserves a day or two to wander about, based perhaps at Keel with its great strand or at Doogort.

The underlying rock is Dalradian: schists and quartzites, with the quartzites forming the highest mountains and the schist dipping steeply to build the needles of Achill Head. Croaghaun needs to be climbed to appreciate its great ridge of cliff, dropping to the sea from a height of more than 600m: not quite so sheer that you feel a risk of falling but you could certainly roll a long way. On the way uphill you pass little tucked-away lakes and you can see down into Keem Bay with its white strand where basking sharks come in and you may find amethysts higher up on the slopes.

To the north of Keel, the long deserted village of Slievemore stands on the slopes of the mountain of the same name. It translates not surprisingly as Big Mountain. The houses were well built of stone and were used until the 1930s as summer dwellings. To the east there are court cairns, commemorating Achill islanders of 5,000 years ago and further on are traces of a model Protestant mission station which flourished in the nineteenth century for a while. The mountain itself lacks the cliffs of Croaghaun but makes a splendid climb to the highest point on the island.

The road from Newport to Achill follows the north shore of Clew Bay, crossing the Burrishoole River by an ancient stone bridge. Three kilometres to the west a road leads off it to the fine old castle of Rockfleet, to which Granuaile retired after the death of her second husband in 1583. While the Nephinbeg mountains to the north of it are barren enough, the lowlands have plenty of freshwater and good land for grazing cattle, to say nothing of the fish and shellfish of a sheltered bay. The coastal strip was a rich man's country in those days.

The road turns inland at Mullaranny or Mulrany where stands a great railway hotel, actually served by a railway until 1934. Mallaranny is the headquarters of the rare Mediterranean heather which grows there to be a shrub of two metres tall. It flowers in early summer, there and over a wide area of Mayo. Achill is reached by a causeway.

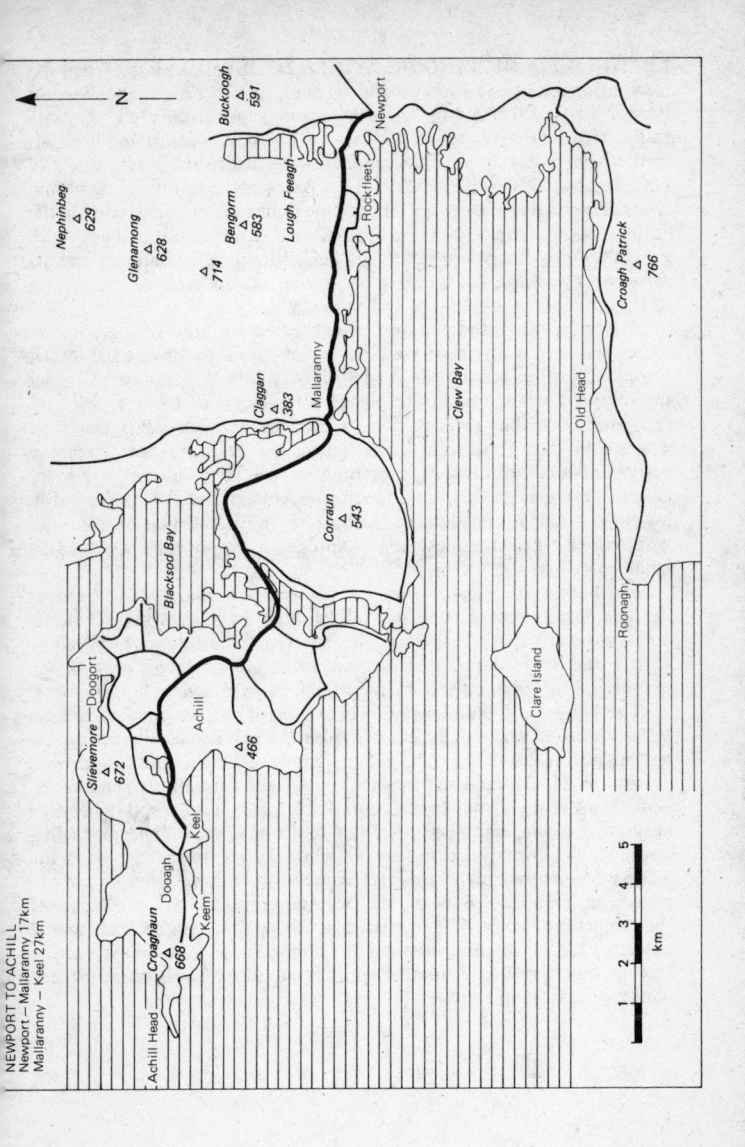

NEWPORT TO ACHILL
Newport – Mallaranny 17km
Mallaranny – Keel 27km

13. THE BOGS OF BANGOR: ACHILL TO BELMULLET

When the Revolution comes, dissidents will be sent to cut turf in the bogs of Bangor Erris. Like Achill it merits many superlatives, but they are rather less inviting. Bangor's bogs are the loneliest, wettest and windiest in the land, interesting for geographers in providing the greatest area of blanket peat, 500 square miles of it. Excessive amounts of wind and weather have eaten away all but the most ancient of rocks, so that the entire region is underlain by Precambrian schists and gneisses, with quartzites providing a magnificent background of Nephinbeg and its western extensions. All too frequently they are hidden by mist and rain so that the level bog seems to roll endlessly away.

The route suggested is a long one, because the land is so poor that there are few monuments ancient or modern to encourage much stopping. A diversion on the road from Achill to Mallaranny takes you round the Corraun peninsula giving a fine view of Clare Island and Croagh Patrick. The geology takes a last look at relatively recent rock where Old Red Sandstone strata appear to the south-east. Then the road heads northwards with bog to either side. This blanket bog is so-called because it grew up as a fairly even covering of the land and follows the original contours in contrast to the raised bog of the midlands which filled in hollows and eventually rose above the surrounding land.

North-west of Bangor you can shorten the journey by heading straight for Belmullet, but the longer road via Carrowmore Lake is much more attractive. It is a big lake, nearly 1,000 hectares, but shallow with a maximum depth of less than 3m. Gulls and terns nest on the islands and tufted duck and pochard flock there in winter.

The village of Belmullet stands by the seaside at the point where the Mullet itself is very nearly cut off from the mainland between Broadhaven and Blacksod Bay. The accumulation of blown sand has allowed pasture to develop and the peninsula has a substantially larger population than the mainland. It is a remarkable place, for long the breeding ground of a small number of red-necked phalaropes, delicate wading birds which properly belong to sub-arctic wastes. It has also been the place where snowy owls, also rare arctic visitors, have most frequently been seen in Ireland. Beneath the bog and gravel in the central part of the Mullet lies rock of Lewisian age, the oldest strata of all in the country. The tip of the peninsula at Termon Point, however, is a rather less ancient granite. Belmullet climate station records some of the windiest weather in Europe.

ACHILL TO BELMULLET
Keel – Mallaranny 31km
Mallaranny – Belmullet 52km
Belmullet – Blacksod Bay 20km

14. NORTH MAYO: BELMULLET TO BALLINA

The full journey is a long one, mainly because there is relatively little to detain a wanderer between Belmullet and Ballycastle, unless a day's walking to see the best of the incomparable cliff scenery is included. From Ballycastle to Ballina the land is richer and there is much more in the way of solid objects to stop by.

A diversion to the north at the crossroads of Barnatra leads around the promontory of Dooncarton where there is a rather delapidated court cairn. The return to the main road passes Pollatomish Youth Hostel. A low, modern building at Glenamoy is the research station for peatland farming run by the Agricultural Institute where methods of turning the blanket bog into fertile land are studied with considerable success. The road north of Glenamoy leads off to Portacloy and Porturlin, tiny fishing harbours where salmon and lobsters provide lucrative employment in the summer. The salmon nets are set at right angles to the coast and capture fish making their homeward journey. Salmon come from great distances to this shore, the record being claimed by a Swedish migrant.

North of Belderg you can look back towards the sea cliffs and you pass the geological boundary from Precambrian schists to Carboniferous sandstones. At Ballycastle civilisation, ancient and modern, begins again. Just to the west of the village is Ballyglass with two court cairns. A diversion to the south-east of Ballycastle leads to the ogham stone, its inscription believed to commemorate a fifth century AD prince and nearby is the thirteenth-century friary of Rathfran together with an assortment of megalithic tombs. To the south Killala's past importance is indicated by the round tower, 26.5m tall, and by the seventeenth-century cathedral.

Two important monastic ruins lie to the east of the road to Ballina. Moyne is a beautifully-preserved Franciscan friary of the fifteenth-century and a little way to the south is Rosserk, also Franciscan and perhaps founded in the same year, 1460. The ease of access to a particularly good run of salmon probably had its influence on the sites of these establishments. They also lie south of the next geological boundary where the sandstone yields to limestone which forms a base for better agricultural land. The great mud flats of Killala Bay are visited in winter by wigeon and thousands of lapwing and golden plover. Ballina, at the head of the estuary, is a thriving town with a large gothic revival cathedral, a pleasing structure when seen from a distance.

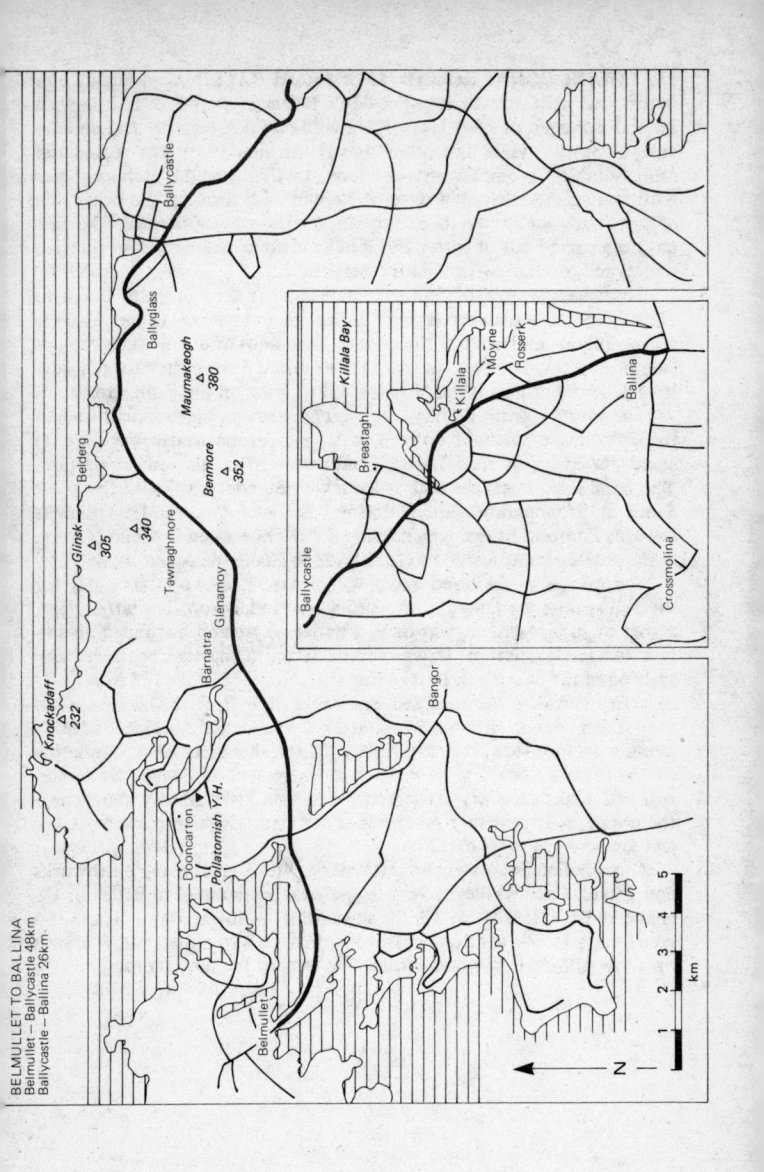

BELMULLET TO BALLINA
Belmullet – Ballycastle 48km.
Ballycastle – Ballina 26km.

15. LOUGH CONN: ROUND TRIP FROM BALLINA

Lough Conn is just the right size to invite a day's journey around it. It follows a general principle of Irish lakes, lying with one side close to acidic metamorphic rocks while the other side is surrounded by the softer and more soluble Carboniferous limestone. In this case the metamorphics are provided by the noble cone of Nephin and, forming the other side of the lonely and lovely Glen Nephin, the Croaghmoyle ridge. The glen has been carved out of softer Old Red Sandstone rock, with Precambrian schists and quartzites forming the heights.

Conn has an area of 5,000 hectares and is deep in parts, down to 28m. Common scoter breed there but the main bird area in the region is the neighbouring Lough Cullin where thousands of diving duck congregate in autumn. The two lakes are rather unusual since they form a side-branch of the nearby River Moy instead of lying on the main stream.

The journey from Ballina southwards needs an immediate diversion to look at the splendid dolmen, with a capstone nearly 4m long. It stands beside a by-road leading south-west from the railway station. The main road meets the lake at Knockmore under a hill with the noble name of Stoneparkbrogan. It follows the lake shore and turns right towards Pontoon Bridge which spans the river between Conn and Cullin. A short diversion towards Foxford leads to a lakeside forest park.

Pontoon is a sheltered spot, where native oakwood struggles for survival against the rampant, if pleasing, rhododendron. The latter plant, a sort of super-heather, was once a native of Ireland but failed to survive the last glaciation. It was reintroduced in the eighteenth-century and found the bog much to its liking.

After Pontoon the road moves away a little from the lakeshore but a diversion back may be made about 2km past Castlehill. This road leads along a promontory to Errew Abbey. It was an Augustinian foundation of the fifteenth-century on a much more ancient site where St Tighernan had a sixth-century settlement. A simple little oratory stands near the abbey, it is probably much older but vigorous restoration work has left few clues as to its date.

Crossmolina is an ancient settlement, with a great many earthworks and graves. Carrowkilleen, 5km to the west on the road to Bellacorrick, is the most extensive of all the megalithic tombs in Mayo. There is a court cairn in the centre and two major burials to either side. It stands on a low hillside in the bog, with a fine view of the mountains.

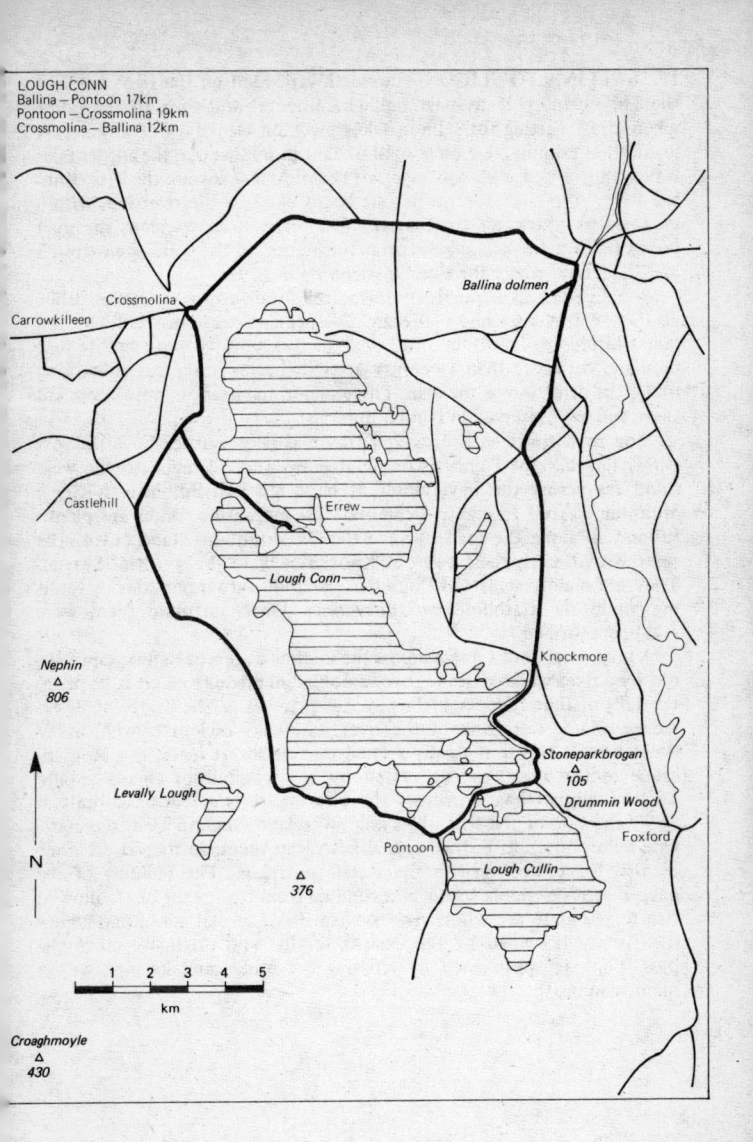

LOUGH CONN
Ballina – Pontoon 17km
Pontoon – Crossmolina 19km
Crossmolina – Ballina 12km

16. BALLINA TO SLIGO

The northward road on the right bank of the Moy estuary leads past Ballina Cathedral and then to the point where draft netting for salmon takes place on weekdays in summer. It is said that salmon were once so abundant in Ballina that the apprentices refused to be fed with too many of them. After crossing the little Bunree River, the road for Inishcrone keeps close to the riverside, with a view across the water to Rosserk. Where the estuary widens the road leaves it for a while and returns at Inishcrone to the wide open stretch of Killala Bay, where the French anchored in 1798.

A side road 2km north of Inishcrone leads down to Castle Firbis, also known by its name of Lecan. The present castle was built by the Mac Fhirbhisigh family in 1560, but for two hundred years before that date and for more than a century after it, Lecan was a seat of learning under the direction of the clan. Three major manuscripts were compiled there and are preserved in Dublin libraries.

The road turns eastwards at Easky and rises a little above the low cliffs. The hills of Donegal, dominated by Slieve League to the west stand far across the bay, closer at hand are Ben Bulbin and King's Mountain. From Easky to Dromore West megalithic tombs are plentiful and all along the road to Sligo the Ox Mountains stand out on the right with their highest point at Knockalongy to the south of Skreen. They are mainly schists of Dalradian age, built into mountains by faulting while the Carboniferous limestones which surround them were still being formed.

Knocknarea looks down across the shallow waters of Ballysadare Bay, fed by a river which cascades over a noble fall made from great horizontal slabs of limestone. A little way downstream of the bridge at Ballysadare on the left bank of the river stands an ancient church, many times rebuilt before it finally settled into decay. It includes a Romanesque arched doorway, decorated by a semi-circle of almost totally defaced human heads. Across the river there is a fish pass, built in 1853 and one of the first of its kind in Ireland. Salmon used to congregate below the falls but were unable to leap them, so there were none to fish for or to breed in the waters upstream. The building of the pass, a series of pools with water running from one to the next, allowed fish to populate the whole river system. By a special act of parliament the fishery is owned by the Cooper family who originally made the pass. Sligo is approached by crossing the bridge and keeping to the main road north.

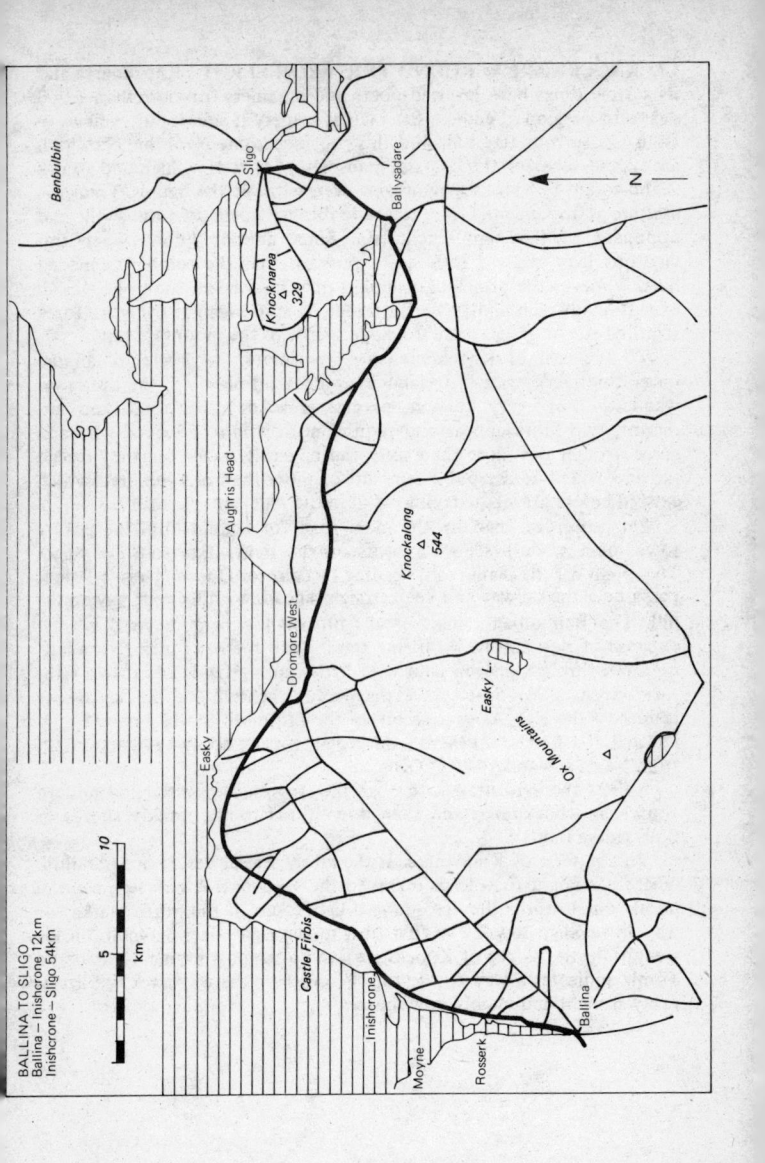

BALLINA TO SLIGO
Ballina – Inishcrone 12km
Inishcrone – Sligo 54km

17. KNOCKNAREA: ROUND TRIP FROM SLIGO Knocknarea and its surroundings have inspired poets and dreamers for more than 4,000 years. In a region of endless spectacular scenery it stands out, well away from the surrounding hills and this provided some Neolithic clan with an excuse to erect the colossal mausoleum. It is 10m high and nearly 200m round but looks magnificent even without the figures. Tradition ascribes it to Queen Maeve, the redoubtable Queen of Connaught and opponent of the hero Cuchullain. Since nobody knows when this vigorous lady reigned it is quite possible that the tomb was indeed hers. Whoever the principal occupant may have been, she or he was an exceptionally rich and powerful leader, able to organise the work force required to hump half a million large stones to the mountain top.

To the east of Knocknarea is Carrowmore, the largest of all the megalithic cemeteries in Ireland. It is a fearful place for the assiduous wanderer. For every dolmen, passage grave or other tomb you surmount, two more appear and require negotiation of barbed wire and gorse. In fact not more than sixty can be easily traced but they spread far and wide and are but a remnant of more than one hundred which existed before gravel quarrying set in in the nineteenth-century.

Set out from Sligo by the main road for Dublin until the yellow tower of a modern school appears on the right, 3km south of Sligo. Turn right off the main road, heading straight for Queen Maeve's Tomb, pass under the railway and keep straight ahead, winding your way up the hill. The Benbulben range spreads out on the right, beyond a great expanse of rich pasture with fine trees. Take the next turn to the left, up a hill through uneven land with little humpy fields and then a right turn which takes you to gravel diggings on the right and the first of the tombs on the left. As you go on up the hill more tombs appear to the left and at a T-junction there is an explanatory signboard and an extract from Yeats's 'Wanderings of Oisin'.

Follow the road straight through the crossroads past the fine modern church at Knocknahar and then downwards to the muddy shores of Ballysadare Bay.

To the west of Knocknarea is the lovely seaside resort of Strandhill, where a straight road leads down to the sea front. An ancient cannon points out towards the ocean and a lighthouse to the north marks the way in to Sligo town. The first turn to the right after Strandhill leads steeply up the slopes of Knocknarea and a signpost saying 'Chambered Tomb' indicates a way to the top. From there the way back to Sligo is fairly straight and mainly downhill.

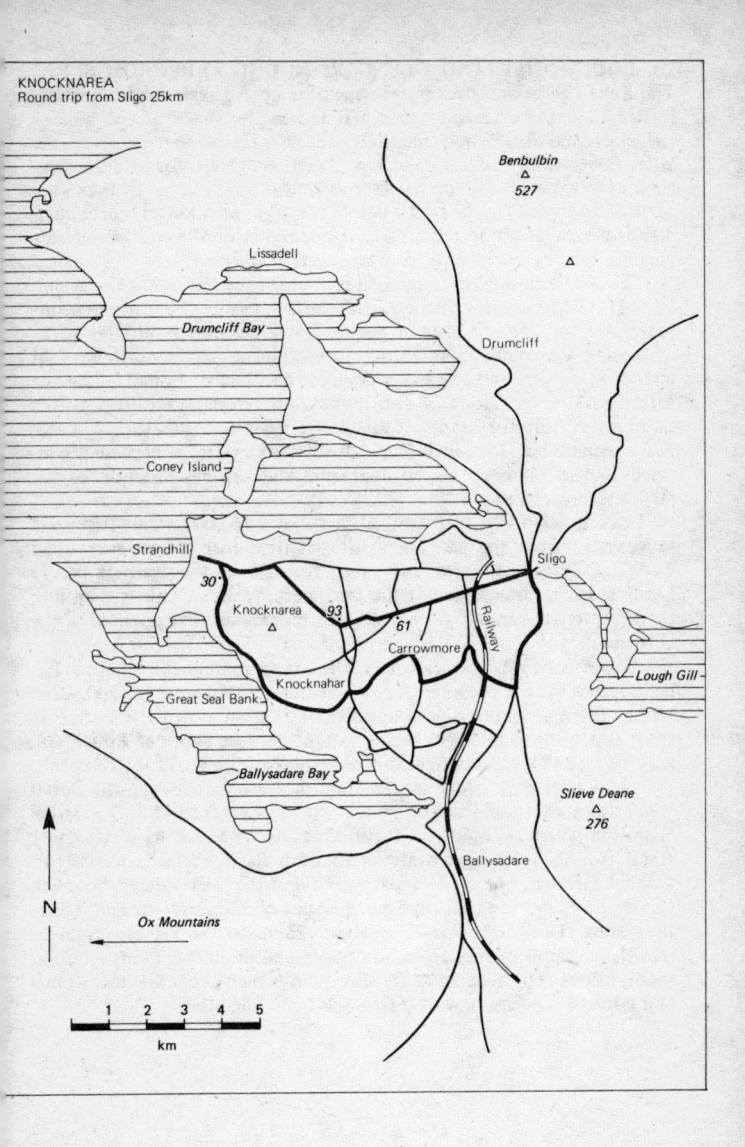

KNOCKNAREA
Round trip from Sligo 25km

18. LOUGH GILL AND GLENCAR: ROUND TRIP FROM SLIGO

The Lake Isle of Innisfree is only one of many highlights in Lough Gill. It lies close to the larger Cottage Island in the shade of the hills of Lahanagh and Slish Wood (Sleuth Wood) near the southern shore of the lake. The beauties of the lake have been recognised for rather a long time before Yeats' day, perhaps for as long as 5,000 years. In the townland of Deerpark on the north side of the lake, up a hill so that it commands a view of the water, an affluent community of Neolithic farmers constructed one of the biggest court cairns in the land.

The southern side of Lough Gill runs along the line of the Ox Mountains fault. Crumplings of the earth's surface before the Carboniferous limestone was formed, caused the ancient Precambrian Moinian rocks of the Ox Mountains to stand out above the land to the north-west. In later times, rivers and glaciers excavated the basin of Lough Gill in the softer rock at the foot of the mountains. Nowadays Lough Gill is famous not only for beauty, Yeats and other obvious features but also has a remarkable flora, including native arbutus which otherwise is confined to the Killarney region in Ireland and belongs properly to the Mediterranean coast.

Leaving Sligo you turn right after crossing the Garavogue River and move away from the lake for a little. A right turn off the main road leads uphill above the lake and passes the signpost for Deerpark before heading downwards again for the lake shore. Parke's Castle was built in the seventeenth-century on the site of a more ancient stronghold of the O'Rorkes.

At Dromahair, Creevelea Friary, the last monastery to be built in Ireland before the Suppression, has survived in a ruined state for 300 years. Within there are interesting scupltures of St Francis in the cloisters. A shortish trip back to Sligo, taking in the Innisfree shore of Lough Gill may be made by turning right off the Manorhamilton road at Dromahair.

The longer way goes through Manorhamilton, following the Bonet River and its floodplain. The remains of the residence of Sir Frederick Hamilton which he built and fortified against displaced natives in 1638 stand to the north. From Manorhamilton the road leads westwards, through Glencar, one of the most splendid of the Sligo valleys, bounded to the north by the cliffs and scree slopes of King's Mountain. Above the valley floor from a level of about 250m to the highest ground a wealth of alpine plants grow, saxifrages and mountain avens amongst many others. The road back to Sligo climbs high above Glencar Lough and later gives a fine view over Drumcliff and Sligo Bay.

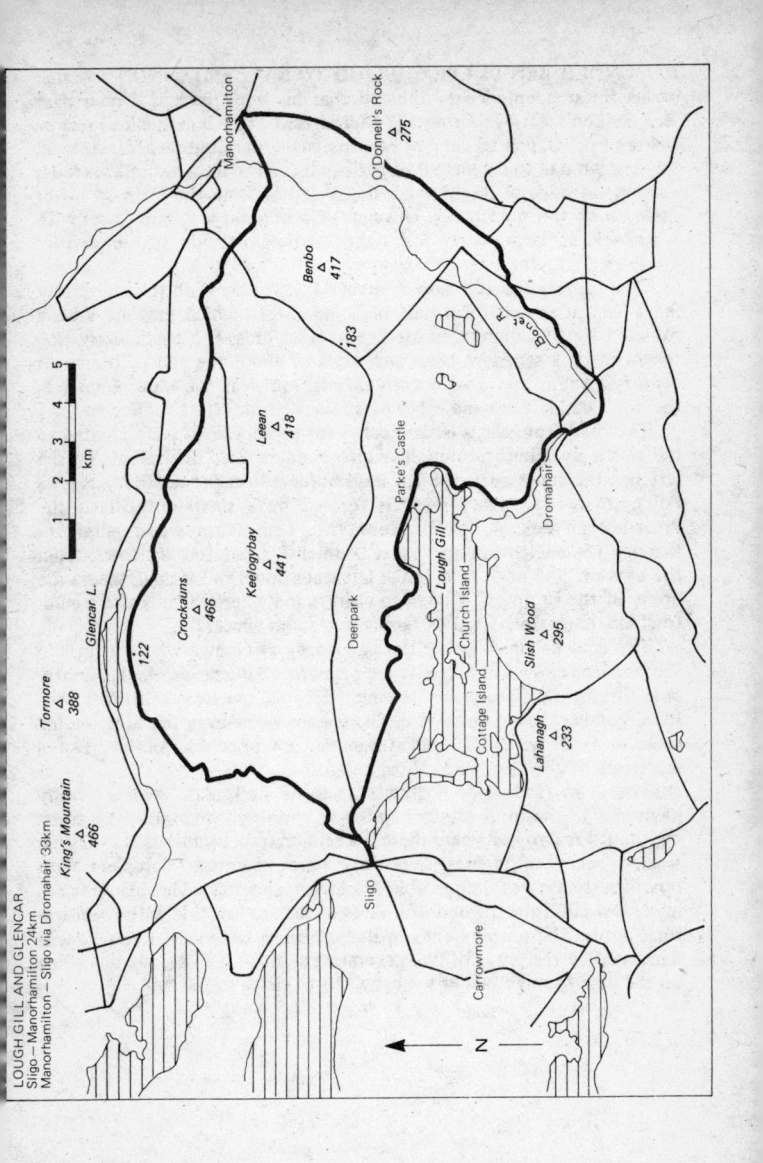

LOUGH GILL AND GLENCAR
Sligo — Manorhamilton 24km
Manorhamilton — Sligo via Dromahair 33km

19. 'UNDER BEN BULBEN': SLIGO TO BALLYSHANNON

In one of his finest poems Yeats directed that his body be laid 'Under bare Ben Bulben's head in Drumcliff Churchyard'. It is a marvellous region, father of poets, painters and politicians, including Countess Markiewicz, the first woman to be elected to parliament. Benbulbin himself is a long, flat-topped ridge of limestone, rising abruptly from the plain of softer shaley rock and sandstones. Drumcliff Church has a square tower with a pinnacle at each corner and stands in the lowlands, surrounded by tall trees.

Two crosses and the base of a round tower pre-date the church by many centuries and form part of a monastery which may have been founded by St Columba himself. The taller cross is a particularly fine specimen of a scripture cross and dates to about the end of the tenth century. Adam and Eve occupy a position near the base, Daniel in the lion's den is there and other personages besides the Crucifixion.

The road from Sligo is signposted for Bundoran. It is dominated to the north by King's Mountain which rises towards Benbulbin. To the left lies the inner part of Sligo Bay, bordered on the north by Rosses Point where the high ground is formed by a small outpost of the Precambrian rock of the Ox Mountains. The main road actually runs through the ancient monastery at Drumcliff, separating the tower from the crosses. The next turn to the left leads down to Lissadell where the home of the Countess is open to visitors and where there is also a wild-fowl sanctuary, inhabited by barnacle geese in winter.

The land becomes rather flat and boggy at Grange where a turn to the left leads down to Streedagh, a pleasant small seaside place, remarkable for the flat limestone pavement beyond the strand, littered with fossil corals of exceptional size. The sea has worn away the surrounding rock so that the corals, called caninia, are exposed, looking like a scattering of grey petrified cabbage stalks.

The main road leads northwest, passing Tullaghan, with a nearby memorial to the Four Masters and then entering Bundoran after crossing the River Drowes where there is a salmon trap. Bundoran is a thriving seaside resort of nineteenth-century railway vintage, complete with boarding houses of impeccable Victorian ancestry. The black shales make low cliffs and a wonderful table of rock at low tide with countless rock pools. The journey ends in Ballyshannon where the River Erne is harnessed by the lower of two generating stations. The zig-zag line going up the dam face is a ladder for baby eels to climb to the top.

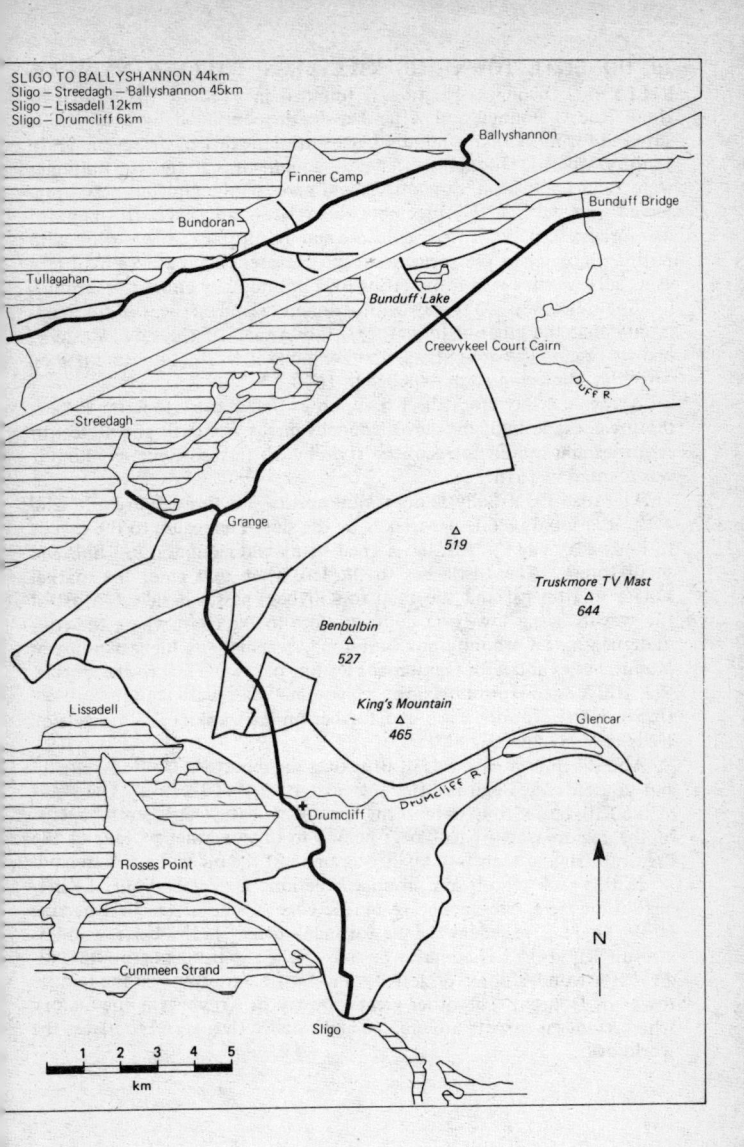

SLIGO TO BALLYSHANNON 44km
Sligo – Streedagh – Ballyshannon 45km
Sligo – Lissadell 12km
Sligo – Drumcliff 6km

20. DONEGAL TOWN AND KILLYBEGS: BALLYSHANNON TO KILLYBEGS

Donegal Friary was founded in 1474 by the mother of Hugh Roe O Donnell and, after her death, continued by his wife. It survived for more than a hundred years until the turn of the seventeenth-century when O'Donnell descendants fought over it and the buildings were reduced to ruin. Some walls and parts of the cloisters stand preserved and within the precincts there is an unusual assortment of memorials: some with fine sculpture and inscriptions, others stark with nothing more than the surname of the deceased. What makes the friary especially worth a visit is its setting on a promontory above the harbour, looking out towards the bay with its many islands. It was in this communty that the great historical text, the 'Annals of the Four Masters', had its origin. The four friars who compiled it wrote it in other places, since the community was expelled in 1600.

Across the Bay from the Friary, on a rock above the River Eske is the great castle built by the O'Donnells in the fifteenth and sixteenth centuries and rebuilt in Jacobean style by Sir Basil Brooke to whom it was granted in 1616.

The road from Ballyshannon runs northwards through drumlin land with occasional reed-fringed lakes by the side. The region to the east of it, known as The Pullans, has a great many lakes amongst low hills and small forests. The castle lies to the left when you enter the market square in Donegal and the road to Killybegs passes beside it. Most of the way is along low-lying country close to the coast where the rock underneath is Carboniferous limestone, reaching its highest point at Mountcharles and with many roads leading off to the left to the seaside. Ball Hill Youth Hostel occupies a one-time coastguard station between Donegal and Mountcharles and further on, at Dunkineely, a diversion leads to McSwyne's Castle.

About a mile westwards of Bruckless the limestone comes to an end and you enter geologically the ancient territory of Donegal. The rocks of the Killybegs Group date to the beginning of the Dalradian Era. Most of the region west of Killybegs belong to this or other periods of the Precambrian and therefore qualify as amongst the oldest land in Ireland.

In this rock a fault has produced the long narrow harbour of Killybegs, allowing a safe anchorage on the edge of one of the best herring areas. There is excellent fishing for many other species besides and as a result Killybegs has come to be one of the top fishing harbours. This gives it a wonderful air of activity and bustle, rare amongst the remote towns of Donegal. The other great industry of Killybegs is the factory where Donegal carpets are created and whence they travel to places the world over.

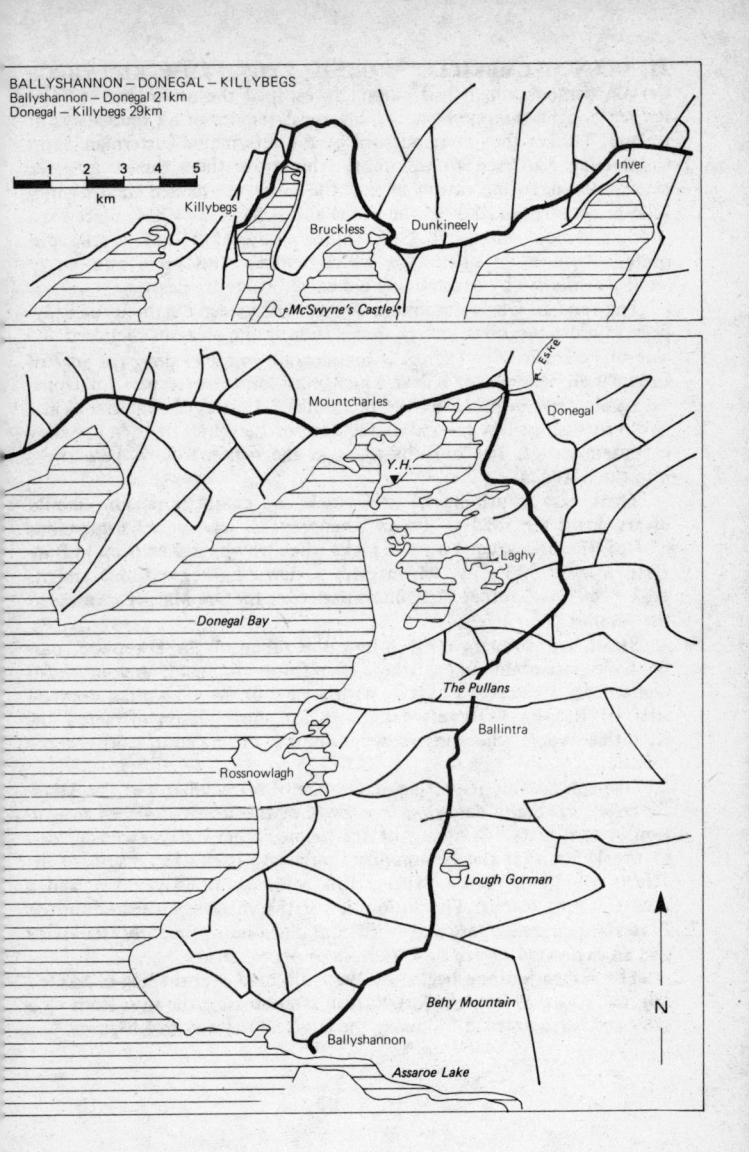

BALLYSHANNON – DONEGAL – KILLYBEGS
Ballyshannon – Donegal 21km
Donegal – Killybegs 29km

21. GLENCOLUMBKILLE: ROUND TRIP FROM KILLYBEGS

Certain demons which had cunningly escaped the attentions of Saint Patrick sought safety in one of the most remote of all the valleys of Ireland. Thither they were pursued by the determined Ulsterman, Saint Columcille, Latinised to Columba, who drove them thence into the nearby ocean. In the course of time the valley was named Glencolumbkille in commemoration of the event and it has been a holy place for a good millenium and a half. St Columba's Day, 15th June, is still celebrated there by a pilgrimage which concentrates on a number of 'stations' marked by exceedingly old carved stone crosses.

The road to Glencolumbkille begins with a steep climb out of Killybegs to cross the ridge and go down again to the pleasant sheltered seaside of Fintragh Bay. Then it is uphill again to travel along the edge of Crownarad, heading for Kilcar which is an important centre for Donegal handwoven tweed. Like the next village, Carrick, Kilcar stands at a river crossing on low ground at the base of the series of barren, shaley mountain ridges. The only by-roads in the region follow these rivers into the hillsides.

There is a youth hostel at Carrick and energetic persons should divert down the road to Teelin whence paths lead to the stupendous cliff of Slieve League. You can make your way by a short step to Bunglass, a mere 300m up, which gives a view of the great cliff and its peak at 601m. A rather vertiginous path over the One Man's Pass leads to the summit.

Strict road-runners must follow the valley of the Owenwee, past its little mountain lakes, where the trout are small, and head for Malinmore, an exposed hillside with a view of the even more exposed islet of Rathlin O'Birne. Malinmore for some reason attracted the Neolithic people who constructed a number of fine court cairns on the hillside.

Glencolumbkille itself shared the fate of many villages of the Atlantic coast, gradually decaying as a result of the steady drain of emigration. A turn in its tide came with the heroic Father McDyer who decided in the 1950s that the community could save itself. The results of his efforts are there to see, with a folk museum, holiday village and a general air of vigour. The antiquities of the village are centred on the Protestant church whose graveyard contains some of the early cross-slabs and an excavated cavern or souterrain of uncertain age.

The return journey begins by the main road over the bog-blanketed hills and down to Carrick. A right turn after crossing the river leads by a hilly and tortuous road following the coast all the way to Killybegs.

GLENCOLUMBKILLE

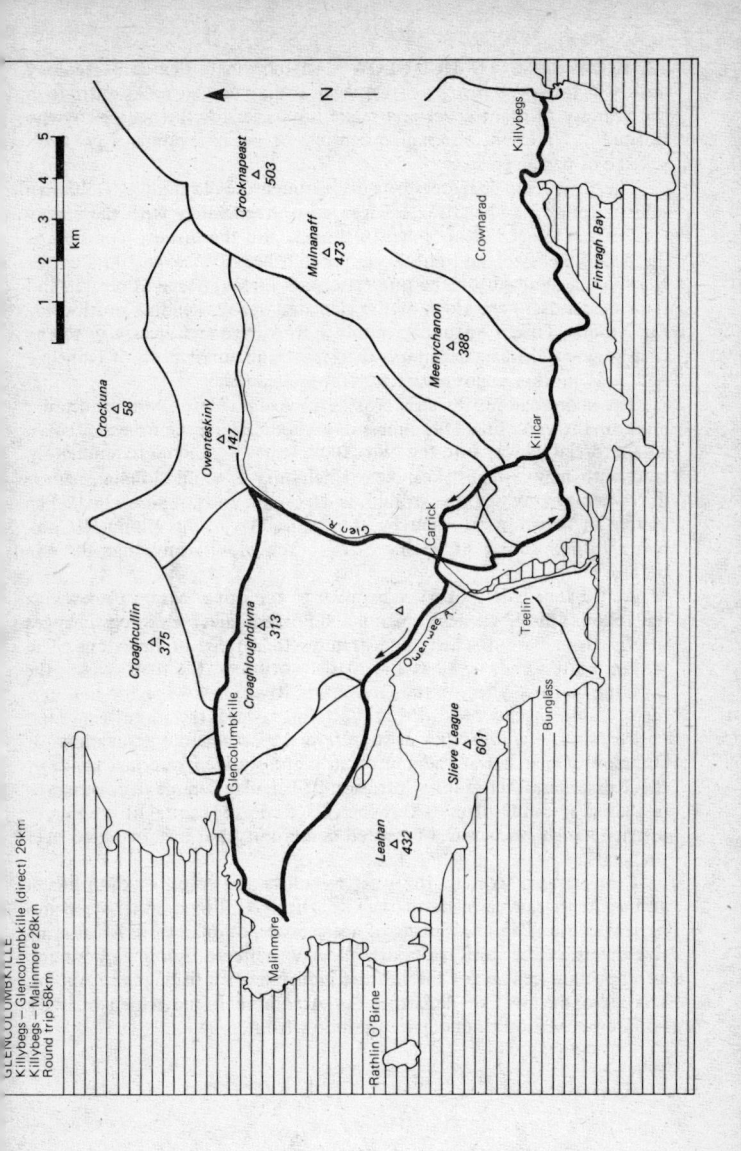

Killybegs – Glencolumbkille (direct) 26km
Killybegs – Malinmore 28km
Round trip 58km

22. KILLYBEGS TO DUNGLOW

An inordinate degree of geology occurs in this western part of Donegal. It may be that rocks obtrude in the scarcity of plant cover and make life easier for the geologists who flocked to the spot for half a century or so, unravelling a complex scheme of past events.

The road from Killybegs sets out through the old familiar Dalradian schists, following the Stragar River up a green valley with the craggy tops of the Crocknapeast ridge to the left and the distant blue hills of the Blue Stacks to the right. It climbs to a height of over 100m at the Neck of the Ballagh on the quartzite rock of Mulmosog Mountain and then descends to the floor of the glaciated valley, heading northwards for Ardara. This is an uncommonly hilly village and gives way to the first view of Errigal Mountain, the tallest and finest peak of Donegal. Ardara is another major centre for Donegal tweed.

The main road northwards crosses the Ardara Pluton, which occupies most of the peninsula. It is a mass of granodiorite, more or less circular, which forced its way into the older rock. It has weathered to undulating land with many small lakes. Near Kilclooney is a fine dolmen, named like a great many of these structures 'Diarmuid and Grainne's Bed'. The couple in question, pursued by the justifiably jealous Fionn McCool, had a dismal choice of resting places, each more stony than the one before.

At Clogher a left turn leads down to tempting seaside places with marvellous sandy beaches at Naran and Portnoo and the geology changes briefly from barren schists and granites to a ridge of limestone. The Ardara Pluton ends at Maas and to the northwest the road crosses the fantastic narrow inlet of the Gweebarra River, following the line of a major fault in the rock. From Lettermacaward the undulating land begins again, rising to 60m or so in several places before descending for Dunglow which lies at the end of an island-studded lake just south of the Rosses, another granite intrusion of singular complexity. Dunglow is a good stopping place, a thriving village and the capital of the Rosses district which once was a crowded community but has dwindled over the years.

Crohy Head, 9km to the west has cliffs and caves, a youth hostel and a circuit can be made of the Croaghegly Hill by a rather steep and narrow route. The hill is made of a succession of quartzites. An alternative diversion goes to Burtonport, a lovely sheltered fishing harbour and an important centre for the herring industry when fishing is permitted. It is also the port of departure for Aranmore Island which boasts a unique population of undersized rainbow trout.

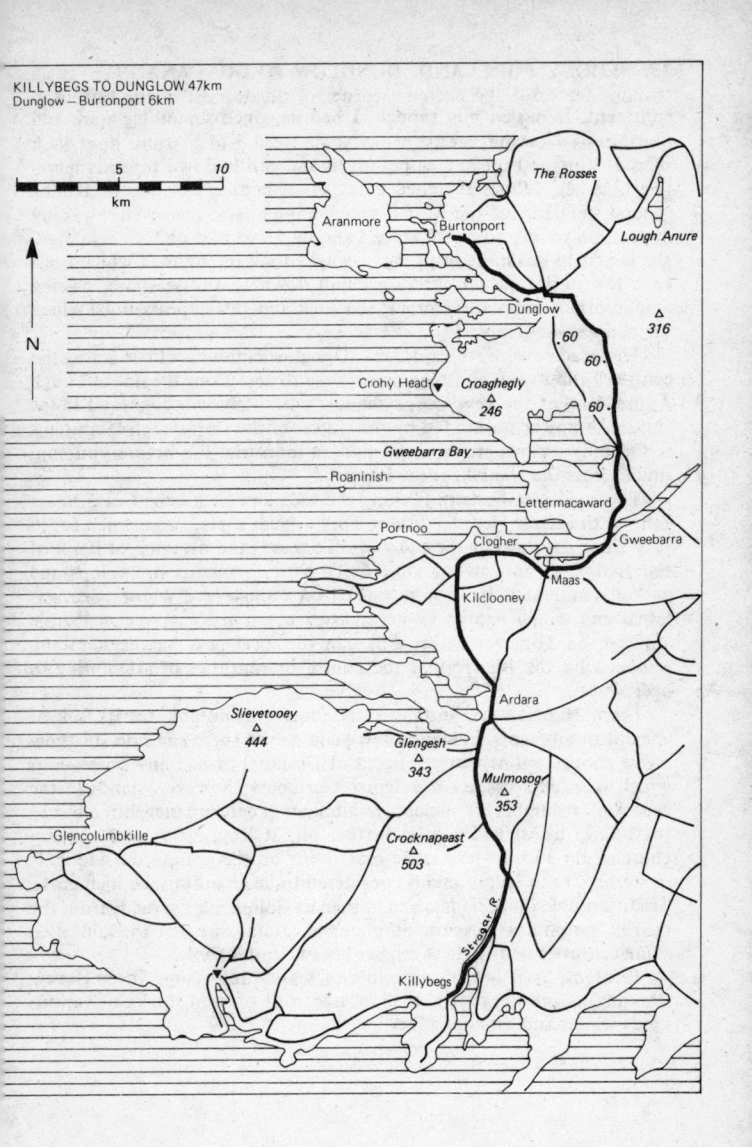

KILLYBEGS TO DUNGLOW 47km
Dunglow — Burtonport 6km

23. BLOODY FORELAND: DUNGLOW TO DUNFANAGHY

It's a striking name for the extreme corner of an outpost of the European continent. It misled me, though. I had imagined something stark and precipitous like the gently named Fair Head which really does look rugged. But the Foreland slopes green and gentle down towards sparkling blue sea. White, thatched cottages sit comfortably on it. By the general standards of the west it seems quite a tame place. That was my impression on my first visit when I simply drove past on the main road. My next trip was more inspiring because I took the by-road which leads to a low cliff top and allows a climb down to the seashore, passing among other things some bright red rock and this appears to be where the name comes from.

The road runs northwards from Dunglow climbing a little across the centre of the Rosses and then descending to pass along the side of Lough Anure, lake of the yew tree, a shallow pool of brown bog water in the granite. A power station fed by the waters of the Derryveagh Mountains is the only serious intrusion of modern industrial life before you continue across the granite for the Foreland.

The road eastwards runs along the hill slope at a height of 50m or 60m with a clear view to distant Tory Island, a place renowned for its fury since the days of the old gods. Tory was the dwelling of Balor of the Evil Eye, an unwholesome deity with characters of cyclops and gorgon combined. He was possessed of a single eye whose gaze was lethal and which had to be kept closed by an artificial eyelid. People still live on Tory somehow, although the local peat has been totally removed by the islanders in the course of centuries of attempting to keep warm.

From Dunglow to Gortahork the journey is notable for its lack of ancient monuments. Evidently few people lived there and none of them made enough money for a spectacular funeral or had any possessions which merited a castle for defence. Gortahork, however, stands in the centre of a number of ancient monuments. There are megalithic tombs to the north-east and a little further on, at Ray, a sixteenth-century church ruin with a great stone cross lying on the ground outside it. It measures 7m in length and is considered to be an unfinished high cross. Tradition holds that no less a man than St Columcille carved it from the nearby mountains. Less romantic persons point out that the saint died some centuries before these crosses became fashionable.

Dunfanaghy is one of a number of seaside resorts on Sheep Haven, standing at the neck of a shallow inlet full of wild ducks of various kinds winter and summer alike.

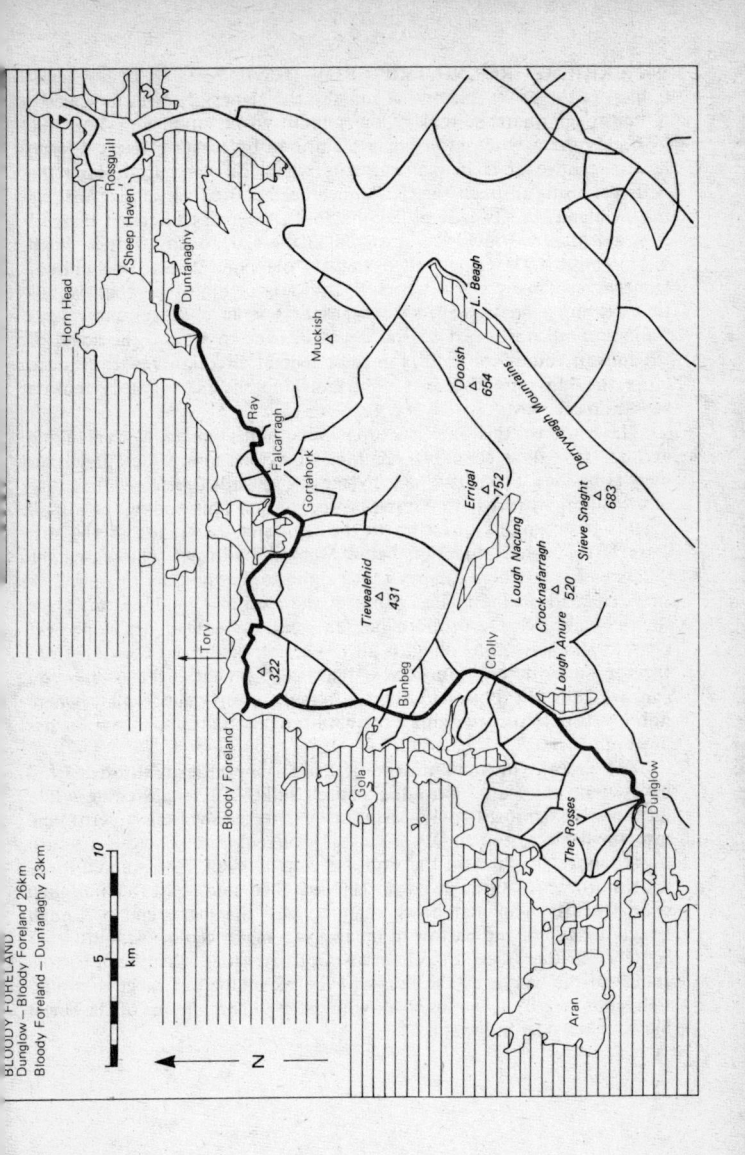

BLOODY FORELAND
Dunglow – Bloody Foreland 26km
Bloody Foreland – Duntanaghy 23km

24. ERRIGAL: ROUND TRIP FROM DUNFANAGHY

Errigal is the noblest of the peaks of Donegal and also the highest. It owes its majesty to the tough quartzite rock of the summit which stood out above the ice fields for a while after being sculptured by earlier glaciers. Errigal lies on a ridge of Dalradian quartzite which can be traced along the Ards Peninsula through the flat-topped heights of Muckish and forming the highlands of Gweedore. To the south of it lies the great mass of Donegal granite which was intruded in the Caledonian period, much later than the Dalradian but extremely old nonetheless. The hills of Donegal were there while central Ireland was a tropical sea-bed. Fantastic earth movements shaped Donegal into a series of ridges and valleys running from north-east to south-west. Roads go around the edges of the hills or follow the valleys in their general direction; few routes can cross the hills and this fact contributes to the marvellously remote sensation they give.

The route on this page is a long and arduous one, really demanding at least two days to allow climbing of Errigal and preferably other heights besides. From Dunfanaghy set out towards Creeslough but turn off to the right just before entering the village. This leads along lowish heights between the quartzite to the right and the granite to the left. Turn left at the T–junction below Muckish and right again along the Calabber River. There follows a long climb to the shoulder of Errigal. A small car park at the highest point of the road is a good starting place for the climb: first over moist bog but soon on a steep, dry slope over heather and scree. The climb is all too breath-taking but the view from the top defies description. Across the road from the higher slopes you can see into the Poisoned Glen, a strange steep-walled valley where nobody lives. No reasonable explanation of its tradition of poison has been put forward.

The descent by road westwards from Donegal leads through Dunlewey with its stark, unroofed church built of the glistening white local marble. Unfortunately, earth movements smashed this superb stone into small pieces too small for masonry or sculpture. There is a youth hostel above the lake on the slopes of Errigal itself. The marked route leads northwards through Falcarragh and then south-east to climb high over Muckish Gap and down again to pass the lower end of Lough Beagh long dark and narrow in the line of a major geological fault.

One of the finest of Victorian Gothic castles, Glenveagh Castle, stands in the woods by the shores of the lake and a vast range of mountain slope nearby is enclosed by wire fence to contain one of the finest herds of red deer in Ireland.

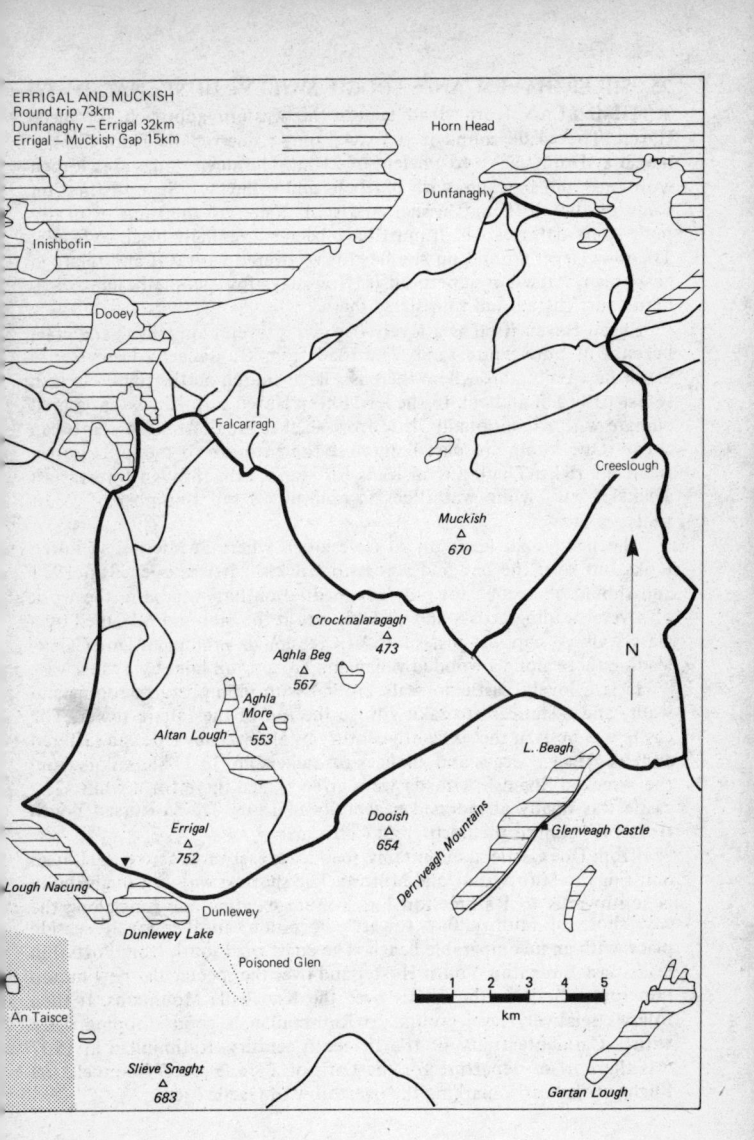

ERRIGAL AND MUCKISH
Round trip 73km
Dunfanaghy – Errigal 32km
Errigal – Muckish Gap 15km

25. SHEEP HAVEN AND LOUGH SWILLY: DUNFANAGHY TO RATHMULLAN

Horn Head guards the western approach to Sheep Haven. The road around it is a steep one, rising rapidly from the salt marsh at Dunfanaghy to a height of 210m. The steep slopes are clothed with grass and bracken, with bluebells and primroses. Seabirds nest on some of the cliffs and in sheltered spots there are the ruins of neatly built stone cottages which must have been exceedingly bleak to live in. The more level ground on the heights is covered with turf and the road gives many views of superb cliffs. Nowadays few people besides shepherds, turf cutters and tourists go there.

Sheep Haven itself is a lovely bay, with several long inlets and great beaches of pure white sand. The road from Dunfanaghy leads southwards past Ballymore where there is a large church on the right and lush forest of beach and oak to the left. Sheep Haven surprisingly has a mild climate with exceptionally little frost so that Mediterranean plants can thrive. One kilometre past Ballymore the entrance to the Ards Forest is on the right. There a road leads for about 3km through forest, past a lakelet with white waterlilies to sand dunes and a number of forest trails.

The main road leads on to Creeslough where St Michael's Church looks out over the bay and across to Muckish. It was opened in 1971 and should be visited not only for meditation but to admire the work of several leading artists and to look out at the mountains framed by a glass wall. A signpost just south of Creeslough announces Doe Castle, leading there along a wooded valley and crossing an inlet by a causeway.

It is a lovely castle to walk around with innumberable rooms and walls, and a staircase to take you to the top of the square tower. The castle was built in the sixteenth-century by McSweeney Doe and suffered endless attacks, sieges and changes of ownership. In 1588, sailors from the wrecked Spanish Armada were given refuge there for a while. The castle was finally abandoned peacefully in 1843. Trá na Rossan Youth Hostel is 16km to the north, past Carrickart.

From Doe Castle, a mountainy road leads eastwards across the Lough Salt ridge to Mulroy Bay and Milford. The shortest way to Lough Swilly is southwards to Rathmelton but a more exciting one runs along the east shore of Mulroy Bay towards Portsalon, another lovely seaside place with an incomparable beach. The coast road south from Portsalon leads past Bunnaton Youth Hostel and over the spectacular new mountain route, built in the 1960s over the Knockalla Mountains. It then follows relatively level ground to Rathmullan, a good stopping place with a Carmelite friary of the fifteenth century. Rathmullan in 1607 was the port of departure for the Earls of Tyrone and Tyrconnell, the Flight of the Earls, marking the overthrow of Gaelic order.

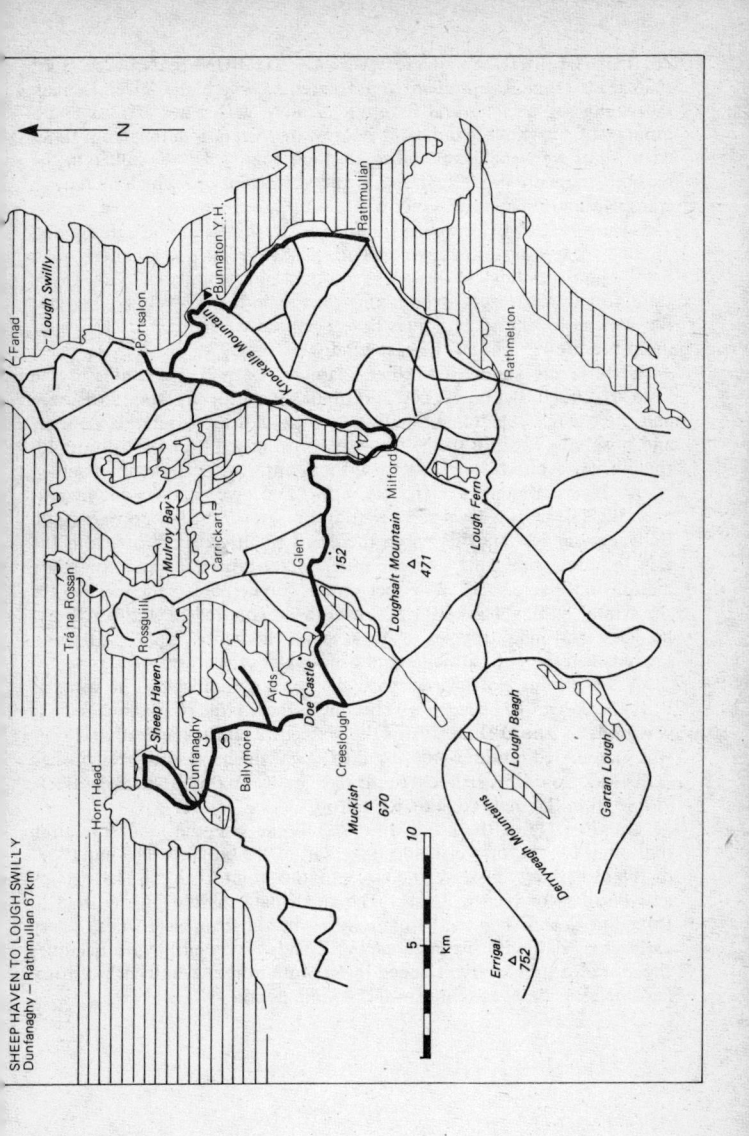

SHEEP HAVEN TO LOUGH SWILLY
Dunfanaghy – Rathmullan 67km

26. LOUGH SWILLY: RATHMULLAN TO BUNCRANA

A coast road leads from Rathmullan to Rathmelton where the River Lennan meets the sea in a natural harbour. A quay with a waterfront and a number of warehouses indicates its past importance, dating from times when ships were shallower and roads more bumpy. Up the hill from the harbour there are modern churches and an ancient one which includes a transplanted romanesque window.

A signpost two kilometres south of Rathmelton indicates Killydonnell Friary and brings you down a narrow road overlooking Lough Swilly and heading downwards through old woodland. The friary stands on a promontory overlooking the lough. It is a lovely setting, but the sixteenth-century buildings have been sadly delapidated. Traces of sculpture survive around the east window.

Letterkenny stands or, rather, clambers up and down hills at the head of Lough Swilly. Its cathedral looks magnificent from a distance and the town is expanding rapidly with new industries, schools, colleges and hospitals. From Rathmelton a left turn at a T—junction continues the journey around Lough Swilly without entering Letterkenny itself.

At Manorcunningham the road rises and gives a view downwards over Big Isle where level fertile ground results from land reclamation. Between Big Isle and the shore there is a small lake, cut off from the tide by a sea wall. This, and the much larger artificial lake at Inch, are major wildfowl resorts. Whooper swans come there from Iceland for the winter and as many as 1,500 have been counted in October. Greylag geese and many species of duck spend the winter months commuting between the two salt lakes and other parts of the Lough.

After turning northwards past Newtown Cunningham the ruins of Burt Castle can be seen on a little hill in the middle of the lowlands. It was built by the O'Dohertys in the sixteenth century and at that time was surrounded on three sides by the Lough which has since been pushed well away from it. A signpost to the right indicates the Grianan of Atlech, visible from the main road on its hilltop.

On the edge of the hill at Burt stands the splendid modern church built in 1967, its form influenced by that of the Grianan. This and other distinguished churches are the work of the architects Liam McCormick and Partners of nearby Derry. The final major shrine on the road to Buncrana is at Fahan in the churchyard by the main road where a very early cross slab with intricate carving stands. The churchyard occupies the site of a monastery founded by St Mura in the seventeenth century and the cross dates roughly from the same period.

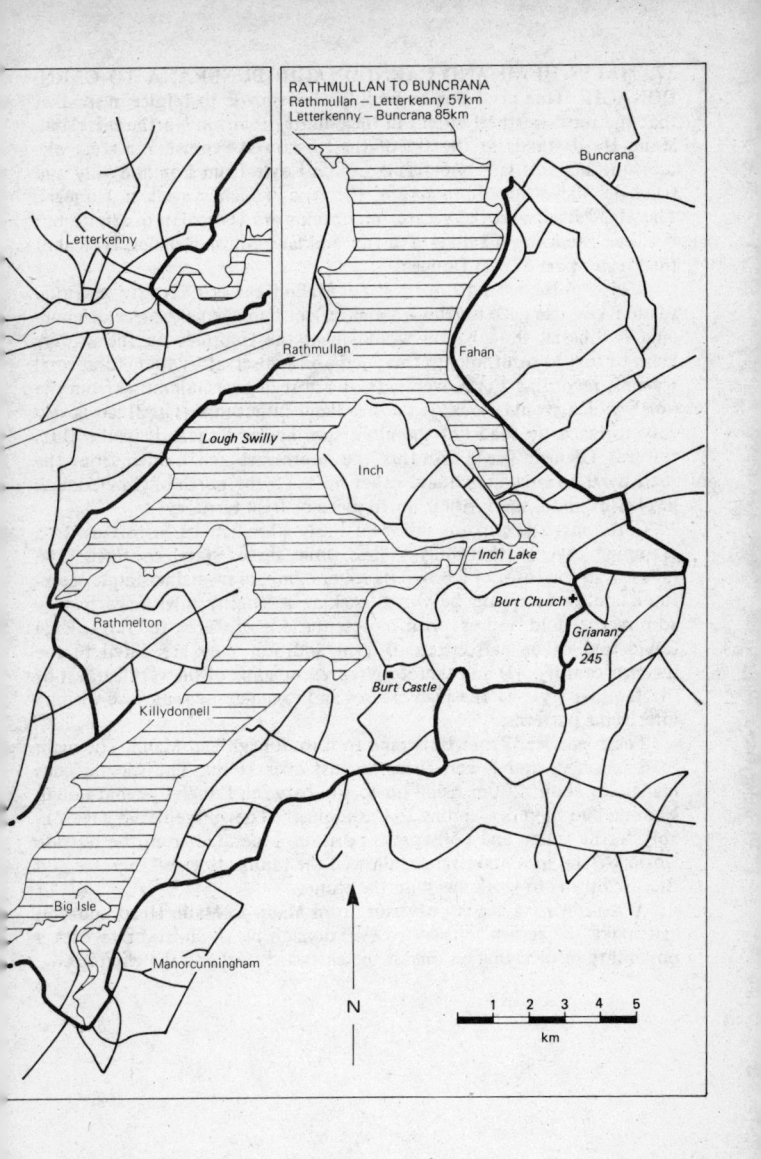

RATHMULLAN TO BUNCRANA
Rathmullan – Letterkenny 57km
Letterkenny – Buncrana 85km

Buncrana
Letterkenny
Rathmullan
Fahan
Lough Swilly
Inch
Inch Lake
Burt Church
Rathmelton
Grianan
△ 245
Killydonnell
Burt Castle
Big Isle
Manorcunningham

N

| 1 | 2 | 3 | 4 | 5 |
km

27. MALIN HEAD AND CARNDONAGH: BUNCRANA TO CARNDONAGH

One need not be unduly chauvinistic to rejoice in the fact that the most northerly point in the country is not in Northern Ireland. Malin Head stands at the tip of the Inishowen Peninsula, a great picturesque mass of land separating Lough Foyle from Lough Swilly and rising in Slieve Snaght to 615m, the second highest peak in Donegal. The Head itself and the greater mountains are Dalradian quartzite but between them lies a valley of softer and later Silurian shales, typical of the greater part of east Donegal.

A visit to the extreme north tip of Malin Head is, of course, essential so that you can gaze northward and reflect that the next piece of mainland is Siberia, though you would meet the Hebrides on the way. A team of rugged ornithologists manned a bird observatory there for several seasons, recording the movements of a host of birds migrating from the north which would flock to the headland in autumn. The Head is also easy to reach by road but the more spectacular scenery is in the cliffs towards Glengad Head towards the south-east and hidden from the road by the Crockalough and other hills. To the north of Crockalough lies Inishtrahull, the farthest north piece of Irish territory.

Carndonagh is a major shrine of Early Christian art historians. In a cramping cage in that hilly village three stones stand confined. The tallest is in the form of a cross, its lesser companions being simple sculptured stelae. It would be worth making a lengthy pilgrimage just to admire the bold and cheerful representations of Christ in Glory, King David and other personages. But in addition they are dated to the seventh century AD and therefore represent some of the very earliest of the familiar style of the high crosses and romanesque sculpture with its interlacing patterns.

The roads lead from Buncrana to Carndonagh and Malin. The main road is longer and lower, rising to just over 100m. The shorter goes higher, to about 200m rising up to run between Lough Fad and Lough Naminn and then descending to Carndonagh. The village lies in a reasonably fertile valley and perhaps its position, separated from the outside world by the mountain range, allowed the monks to dwell in peace and their sculptors to work away on the stone.

A seaside road leads outwards from Malin to Malin Head and you can make the return journey to Carndonagh by the inland one with a possibility of diverting on one of the eastward tracks to the clifftops.

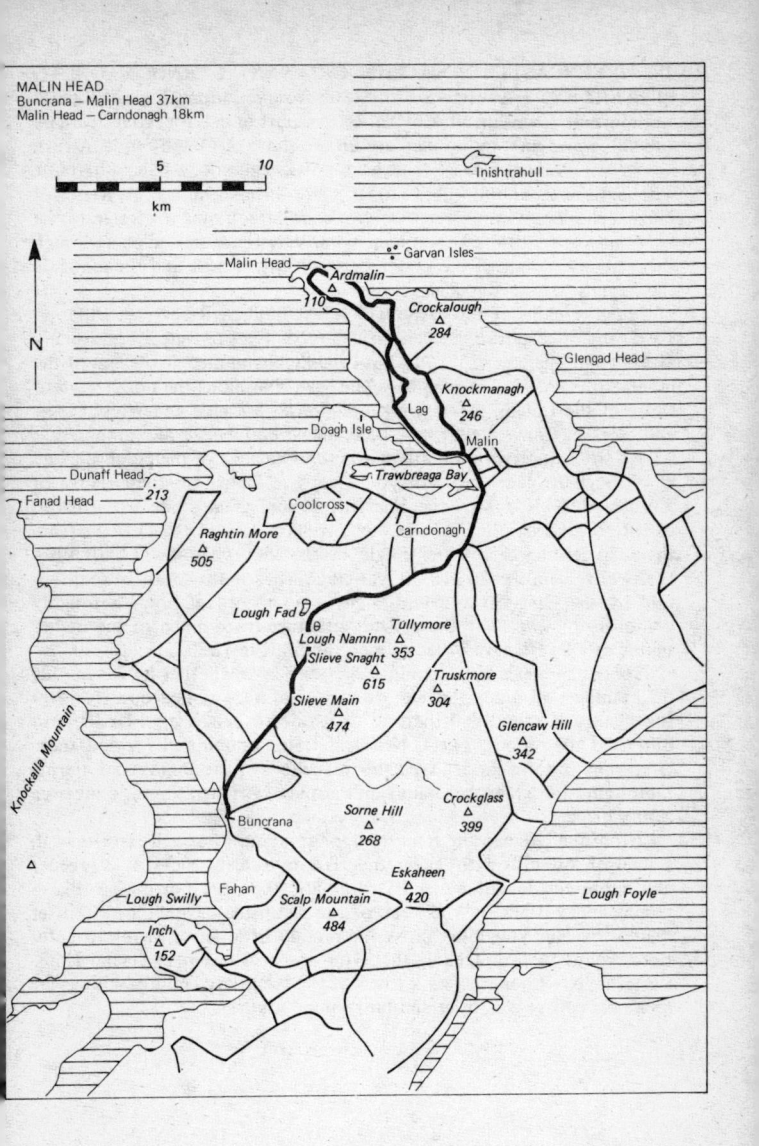

MALIN HEAD
Buncrana – Malin Head 37km
Malin Head – Carndonagh 18km

28. GREENCASTLE AND THE GRIANAN: CARNDONAGH TO LETTERKENNY

A westward road leads from Carndonagh to the slightly unimportant township of Moville, once a port of call for Atlantic liners and still a pleasant stoppping place on the shore of Lough Foyle. A turn to the left along the coast road leads to Greencastle, a fishing harbour with a fishery school where students are initiated in the mysteries of radar, echo-location, power blocks and other equipment foreign to the fisherman of tradition. In summer, salmon by the thousand pass through the narrow opening of the Lough between Greencastle and the fantastic flat expanse of the Magilligan.

Much remains of the castle which was built by Richard de Burgo in 1305 and incorporating even earlier work. It survived a great many attacks and changes of loyalty until finally abandoned at the end of the nineteenth century. Turning back the road runs along the north-western shore of the Lough, passing in succession Red Castle and White Castle and reaching Carrowkeel where there are several megalithic tombs.

At Muff the road goes inland to cross the neck of the peninsula and go through Bridge End until you meet a signpost for the Grianan of Aileach. This is one of the finest of several great stone forts placed usually on hilltops or cliffs. It was a royal palace of the O'Neills from the fifth century AD, which might be the time when it was built, until the twelfth century. In 1101 it was demolished in the course of a reprisal raid by the King of Munster. There is no record of how thoroughly demolished it was but the present structure owes much to the undertaking of a Dr Bernard of Derry who rebuilt it in 1870.

So the modern visitor cannot be quite sure whether he is standing on a rampart of millenial age or on a piece of Victorian vigour. However the history is sound and there is no reason to believe that Dr Bernard imported the stones. The O'Neill chieftains undoubtedly stood there from time to time and enjoyed the marvellous view of blue water, purple mountains and green headlands and islands. 'Grianan' literally means a sunny place.

From the Grianan the road for a long way runs through east Donegal, a land of low hills with lakes, underlain by schisty rocks. It is greener and more fertile but much less dramatic than the north-west. Place-names and villages on the neck of the peninsula have an air of Ulster Plantation and you must cross the muddy little River Swilly to enter Letterkenny before feeling that you are back again in Gaelic lands. Letterkenny is nonetheless a town of the twentieth century with a fine technical college, factories and burgeoning suburbs.

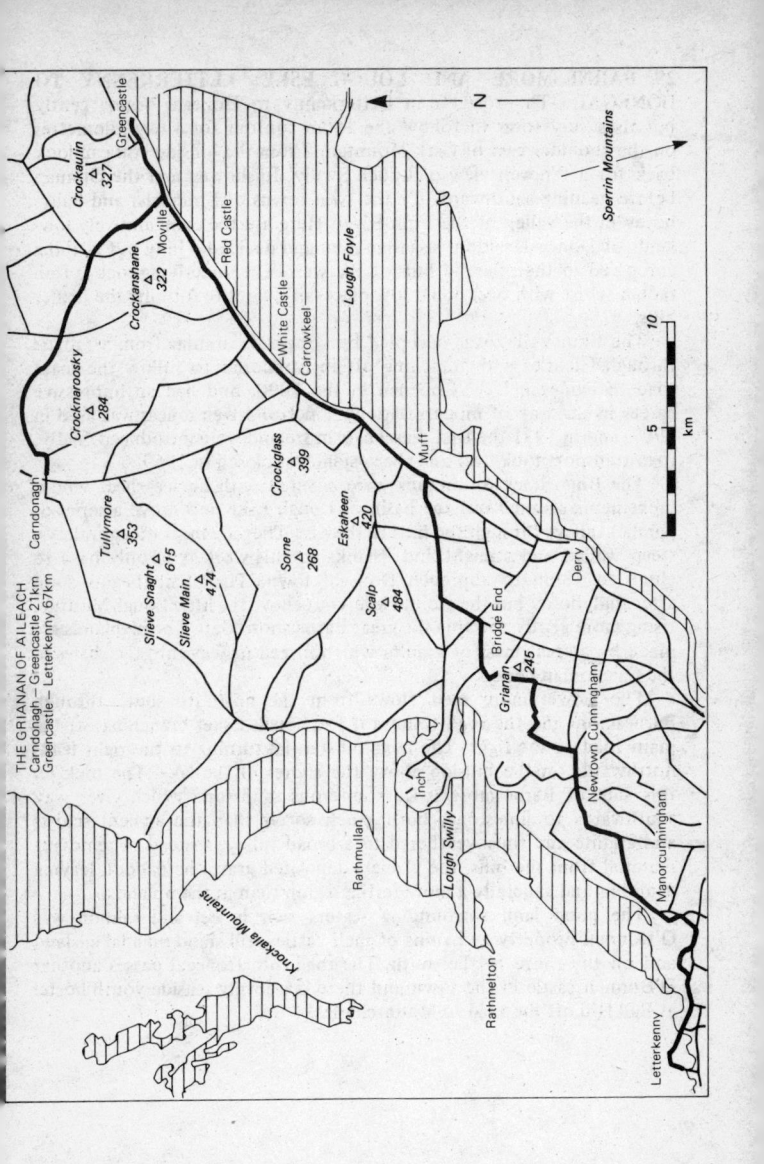

THE GRIANAN OF AILEACH
Carndonagh – Greencastle 21km
Greencastle – Letterkenny 67km

29. BARNESMORE AND LOUGH ESKE: LETTERKENNY TO DONEGAL

The road from Letterkenny to Donegal begins gently but rises very soon to follow the 150m contour for a few kilometres on the shoulder east of Cark Mountain. From the hillside you can look back for a farewell view of Lough Swilly, Inishowen and the Grianan before heading southwards for the twin towns of Stranorlar and Ballybofey in the valley of the Finn River. Here are the comparatively lowlands of Donegal, seldom less than 60m and decidedly hilly but nothing compared to the splendid hills of the west. The underlying rock is Dalradian schist with occasional lost pieces of quartzite forming the higher hills.

The Finn Valley was occupied by a railway, running from Strabane through Glenties and branching off in Stranorlar to follow the main road to Donegal. It was opened in the 1890s and had an impressive career in the way of modernisations: a petrol-driven railcar was used in 1907, and in 1931 the first diesel cars in Ireland were introduced. Sadly, road transport took over and the system was closed in 1959.

The Blue Stack Mountains were covered with an ice sheet whose movements scoured out the basin of Lough Eske and drove a series of parallel valleys through the hills to the east. They are magnificent valleys, steep walled and straight and, thanks to this work, you only have to climb to 180m to approach Donegal town. The climb begins soon after Ballybofey but the ground levels out above the little Lough Mourne, rising more gently towards the great Barnesmore Gap. The highlands are made by a great mass of granite which forced its way into the shales in the Caledonian period.

The Lowerymore river flows from the north to south through Barnesmore and the road follows it for Lough Eske, branching off the main road to the right. The next substantial turning to the right leads northwards on the hillside above the shores of the lake. The rock on this side of Barnesmore is Carboniferous sandstone which gives way southwards to limestone, both much softer than the ancient schists and granite and thus weathered to a broad valley. Instead of removing material from the hills, the glaciers deposited gravel hereabout, leaving drumlins and generally a more fertile region than in the uplands.

The good land surrounding waters rich in eel and salmon was O'Donnell property and ruins of their castles still stand on a lake island and on the shore to the south. The road into Donegal passes another O'Donnell castle in the town and there is a lovely seaside youth hostel at Ball Hill off the road to Mountcharles.

LETTERKENNY TO DONEGAL 55km

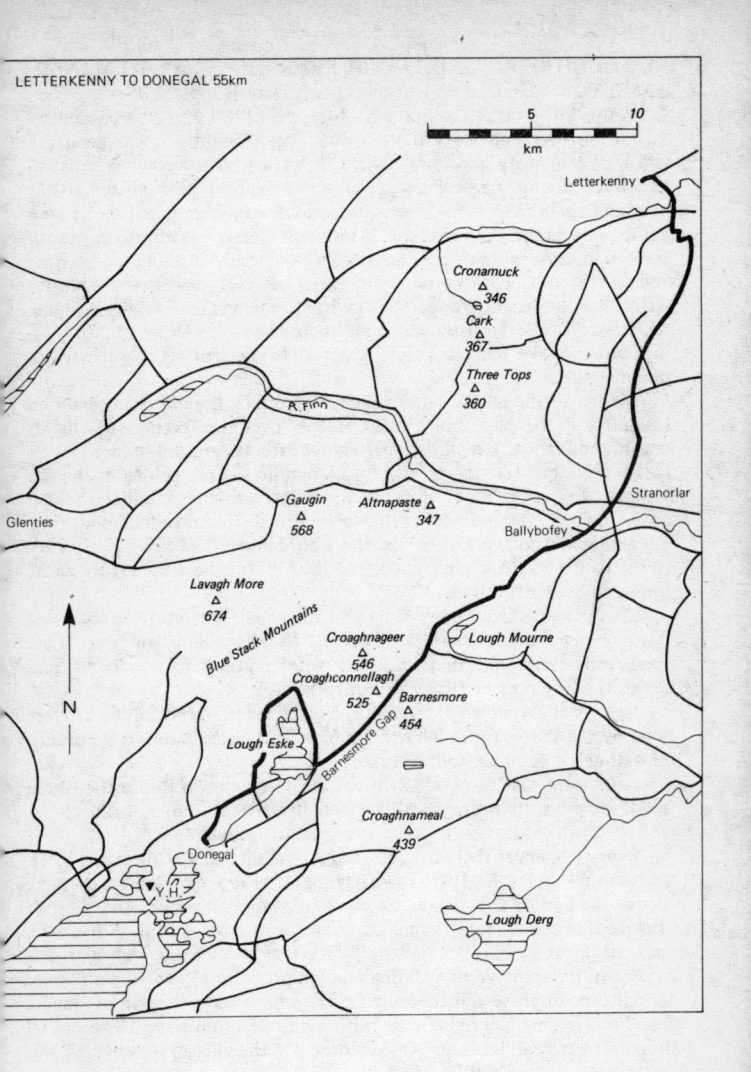

30. LOUGH DERG AND LOUGH ERNE: DONEGAL TO MANOR-HAMILTON

From time to time Lough Derg is a place of pilgrimage. A lovely, lonely lake set amongst forested hillsides, it was chosen by St Patrick to spend forty days fasting. Upon Saint's Island he had a vision of purgatory and 'St Patrick's Purgatory' has been an alternative name for the site. Since mediaeval times pilgrims have visited it but now and again their behaviour was considered unseemly and the church authorities banned the exercise. At present well-behaved pilgrims travel thither in cars and subject themselves to a severe discipline of fasting and meditation. To accommodate them the great basilica on Stations Island was built and consecrated in 1931. The Italian-looking building which overflows the little island looks strange in the Donegal surroundings but the lake with its placid water and reflections is able to accommodate it.

A turn to the left off the main road from Donegal to Ballyshannon heads for Pettigoe, climbing quite steeply over the shoulder of Oughtdarnid and then remaining on high, heathery ground underlain by rocks described as 'flaggy siliceous granulites' and belonging to the Moinian Era, even older than the incredibly ancient Dalradians which cover most of Donegal. What matters more to the traveller is that they are acidic and in the context of the wet climate yield poor, peaty soils so difficult to earn a living from that the hills remain amongst the most lonely in the land.

To the south lies Lough Erne and the road leads into the village of Pettigoe whence north to the lake. A diversion along an unmetalled road leads farther north to a lovely woodland where the River Derg leaves the lake on its journey to Lough Foyle.

Near Pettigoe you can cross into Northern Ireland to follow a lovely road by the shores of Lough Erne, looking across the water to the superb limestone cliffs on its southern shore.

It may be well to check with the local Customs or Police that these roads are permitted. You cross the Erne in Belleek, source of fine china, and so southwards passing the eastern end of Lough Melvin.

From Rossinver there is a relentless climb up Saddle Hill, rather bleak and damp-looking land with a scattering of sheep and rarely a cottage. From the Saddle the distant view is of flat-topped mountains, a range unnamed on the maps, which separates you from Lough Allen. The lack of great houses on these hillsides is very striking, the land was probably not capable of yielding enough profit to pay for the building. Conditions improve a little down in the valley and the town of Manorhamilton is now a thriving one, with many new bungalows. The ruined home of the founder Hamilton stands above the village, ivy-covered and castellated. It was built in 1638.

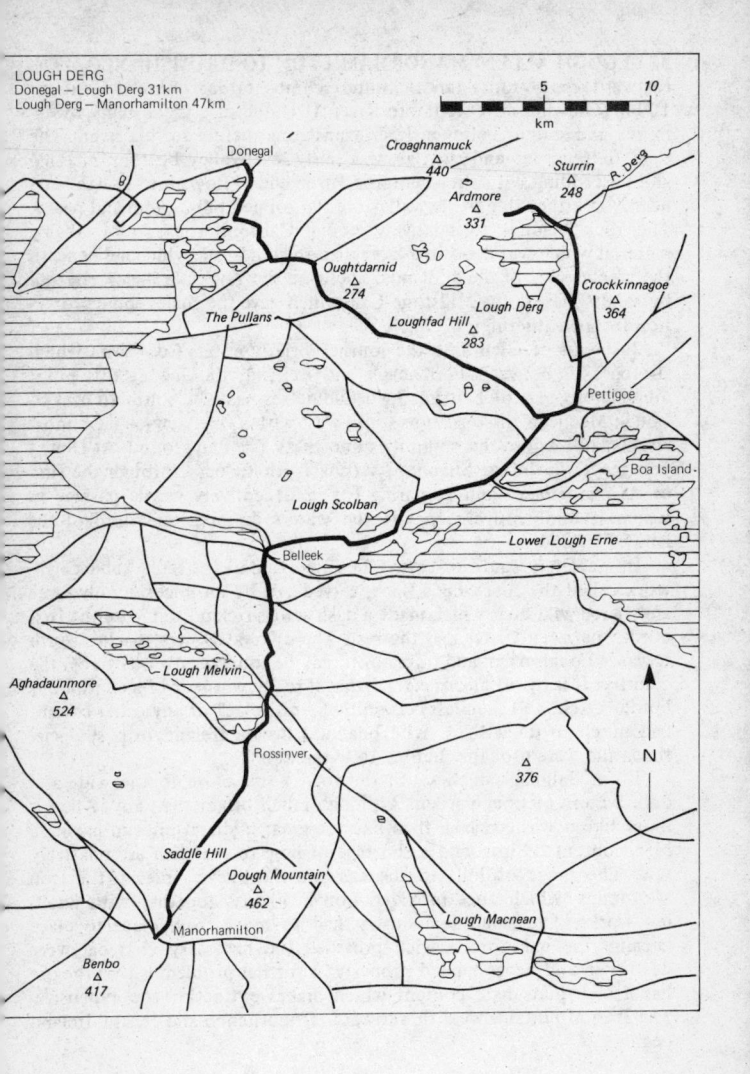

LOUGH DERG
Donegal – Lough Derg 31km
Lough Derg – Manorhamilton 47km

31. LOUGH ALLEN: MANORHAMILTON TO DRUMSHANBO The eastward road from Manorhamilton climbs rather quickly to about 100m following an Owenmore River. It is one of a great many owenmores and sounds better in Irish, translating merely to 'big river'. The road flattens out and runs along a fairly level valley bottom, meeting and descending with the Glenfarne River which flows into Lough Macnean. On either side of the valley are flat-topped hills, damp and peaty. The rock belongs to relatively young Carboniferous strata, shaley material which was deposited later than the limestone which lies beneath the greater part of the midlands. These are the Yoredale shales, covered by sandstones of the Millstone Grit which gave the shales some protection from weathering.

Just east of Glenfarne the journey briefly enters Co. Cavan which stretches in between Fermanagh and Leitrim, looking at this point much more part of Leitrim. Two kilometres past the southern arm of Lough Macnean the road runs south-west with a fine view of the almost circular hill whose flat summit is known as The Playground. At Dowra you meet the infant Shannon, setting forth to pass through the first of its major lakes and preparing for its deceptively gentle passage in which it unobtrusively engulfs the waters draining one third of the land of Ireland.

Immediately south of Dowra lies a portion of the remarkable earthwork called the Black Pig's Race, carved out by an uncommonly large and fierce wild boar which made a dash across Ireland to create the first border between Ulster and the rest. The dyke at Dowra reaches south towards Lough Allen and traces of it may be found eastwards across the country. It is by no means certain that it really was part of a continuous border ditch, and even less certain that a pig, black or any other colour, had much to do with it. Wild boar did live in Ireland in post-glacial times and were probably hunted to extinction.

From Ballinaglearagh south the road keeps close to the wide and dark waters of Lough Allen. Although much bigger than any, Allen is more like a western lake than like the great midland ones in having a high content of iron and a shortage of lime so that fish are relatively few. The range of hills to the east are the Slieve Anierin, the Iron Mountains, which once provided iron in plenty, together with smelting works. The smelting industry had to move from place to place because the oak forests wich provided the necessary charcoal were destroyed and never tended properly. A further problem is that the ore has a high phosphate content which makes extraction too expensive. The Iron Mountains wear thin towards Drumshanbo and central Ireland begins.

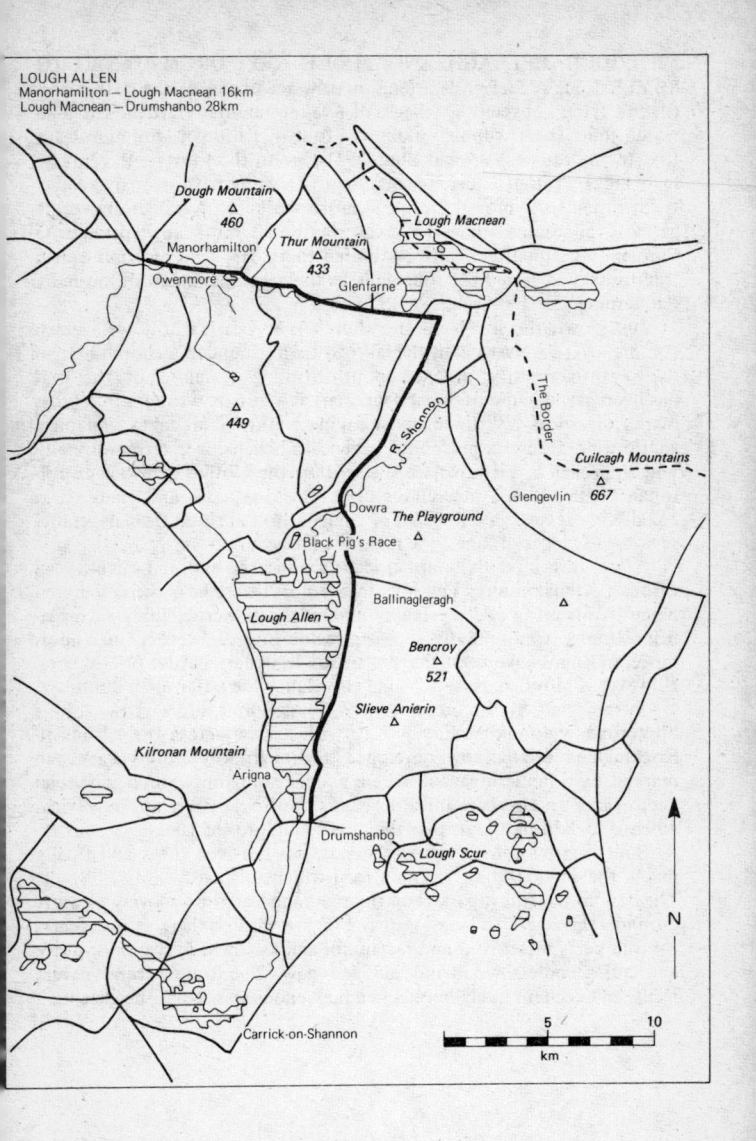

LOUGH ALLEN
Manorhamilton — Lough Macnean 16km
Lough Macnean — Drumshanbo 28km

32. LOUGH MEELAGH AND LOUGH KEY: DRUMSHANBO TO BOYLE

Lough Meelagh is a long, narrow reed-fringed lake with many islands, lying between the villages of Keadew and Ballyfarnan. The road which joins them running along the foot of Kilronan Mountain leads first to the ruined Kilronan Church. Dating to the fourteenth century, it includes a rather unusual romanesque doorway with strongly geometrical ornaments, moved from an earlier building. A tablet above the gateway announces that the great traditional musician, Turlough O Carolan, who died in 1738, was buried there. His wake was more than traditional and lasted for four days to the accompaniment of music by ten harpers.

Just down the hill from the church is St Lasair's holy well which commands a lovely view of the lake. St Lasair founded a church here in the seventh century or thereabout. Nothing remains but the well has been paved and covered and a remarkably ornate wrought iron cross marks the spot. A little signpost saying Nature Trail takes you on a gentle walk around a promontory beneath lichen-covered trees. Finally you approach a picnic place just within the Gothic gateway of Kilronan Castle. It is a marvellous piece of stone work and leads to an equally impressive gate lodge, now ruined. Both are built from naturally-sculptured pieces of limestone from the lakeside.

A left turn after Ballyfarnan leads around the end of Lough Skean through Kilmactranny. The hills to the north-west bear the celebrated name of Moytirra and the region abounds in rather delapidated megalithic tombs. Undoubtedly it was a region of great wealth and importance and may have been the site of the legendary battles of Moytirra. However, a Moytirra close to Cong also claims the latter distinction.

Turning left at the crossroads of Corrigeenroe brings you along a hilly road overlooking Lough Key with a view across the islands to Rockingham estate, now developed as Lough Key Forest Park and marked by a modern gazebo where a great house once stood. The road keeps close to the lake until it crosses the Boyle River at Knockvicar where a lock brings boats past the rapids and into the lake.

Southwards of Knockvicar the way lies between lakes and finally meets the main Dublin to Sligo road which runs westwards to Boyle. The gate to the forest park is on the right and leads into a lovely pleasure ground, catering for most tastes. For the masses there is a carpark, caravan park, waterfront and restaurant and for those in search of peace and quiet endless woodland old and new. There are several nature trails, an excellent guide book and a marvellous view from the gazebo.

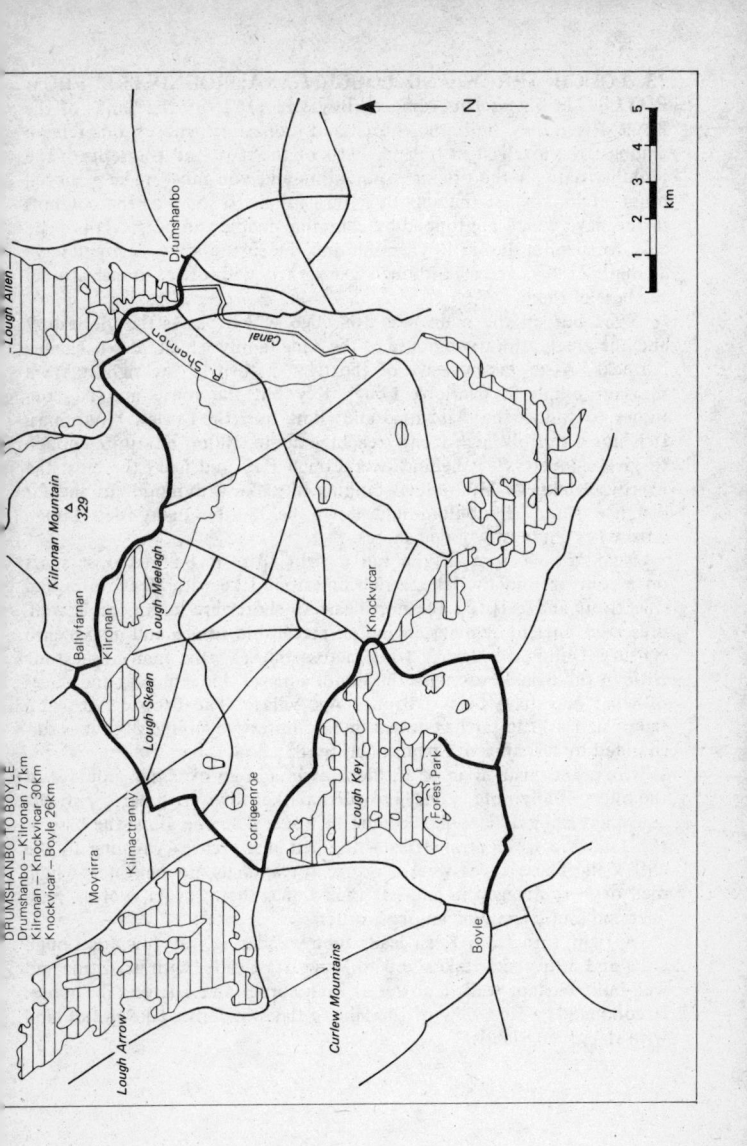

DRUMSHANBO TO BOYLE
Drumshanbo – Kilronan 71km
Kilronan – Knockvicar 30km
Knockvicar – Boyle 26km

33. LOUGH ARROW AND LOUGH GARA: ROUND TRIP FROM BOYLE

The Cistercians came to Boyle in 1161. By the banks of the Boyle River they built the church and monastery whose ruins remain amongst the loveliest in Ireland. Parts of the nave and transepts of the building date to the original foundation and you must make a special point of looking at the slightly later capitals to some of the columns in the nave which are topped by charming people and beasts. It is quite easy to spend a day in Boyle itself and the surroundings really deserve a couple of days at least although a single trip will suffice to rush around the best of them.

Start out on the main road for Sligo which passes the monastery and the great, grim town house of the King family which later became a barracks. After taking leave of the river, a turn to the right takes a pleasant climb to overlook Lough Key but the route marked continues to follow the main road and climb over the Curlew Mountains. It is not a terribly high climb, reaching about 200m, but quite enough to give a lovely view behind over Lough Key and from the crest the nearby Bricklieve Mountains standing out like a pyramid. In the far distance stands Benbulbin and down below the many-isled Lough Arrow lies amongst wooded shores.

Near the bottom of the hill a right turn at Ballinafad sets off on a tour around the lake, a rich limestone lake with clear water and fine trout and eels. By the north-eastern shores are innumerable well-preserved ancient remains including megalithic tombs and a sixteenth century Dominican friary; while across the lake the many limestone cliffs of the Bricklieves mark the site of a megalithic cemetery and traces of what may have been a Bronze Age village. The Bronze Age cairn signposted a little farther on is a most impressive mound of stones surrounded by less ancient Spanish chestnuts.

Cross the main road at Castlebaldwin and go over the shoulder of the hills to Ballymote, a busy crowded market town with narrow streets and many shops. Signposts leading to Boyle take you along the base of the fantastic Keshcorran Hills with their many caves yawning in the cliff wall. These caves were a refuge for animals, now extinct, which died or were dragged in and left their bones there: bears, wolves, reindeer and arctic lemming amongst others.

A right turn from Kesh leads by a wandering way towards Lough Gara and a diversion takes you to Moygarra Castle, with its strong and well-built curtain wall, a tower at each corner and a large gate house. It commands a fine view of the lake, a flat wandering lake in flat land with flat green islands.

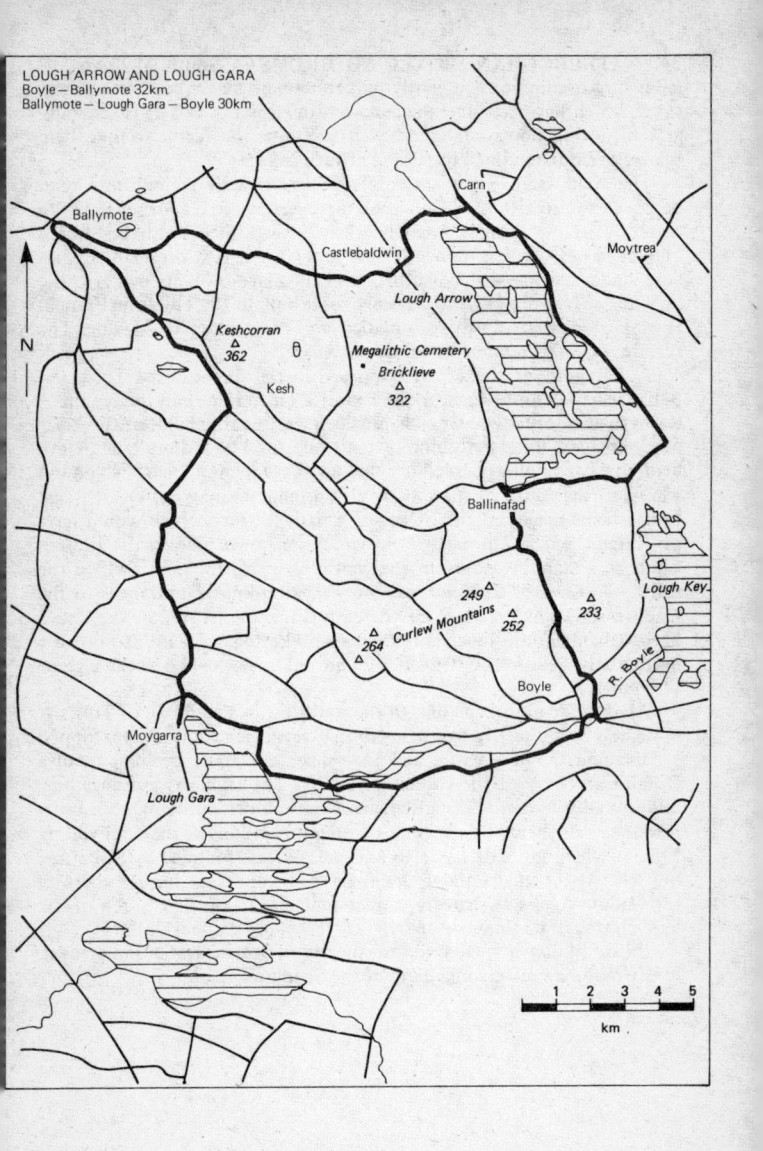

LOUGH ARROW AND LOUGH GARA
Boyle – Ballymote 32km.
Ballymote – Lough Gara – Boyle 30km.

34. RATHCROGHAN: BOYLE TO DRUMSNA

South of Boyle the lands of Roscommon are gently hilly, underlain by Carboniferous limestone which has been liberally spread with glacial gravels. It is generally green land but poorly drained and hence none too fertile so that there is a lack of outstanding houses and affluent estates.

The road from Boyle sets off southwards with a climb and then descends to cross the floodplain of the Breedoge River for several kilometers of damp flatness. Frenchpark is distinguished as the birthplace of Douglas Hyde, the pioneer Celtic scholar and first president of Ireland under the present constitution. The village owes its name to the fact that it grew up close to a stately home built in 1729 by John French. It was a splendid dwelling but died and decayed in the 1950s. The remains stand to the northwest of the village.

A left turn at the crossroads leads in the direction of Tulsk. At Bellanagare it climbs to near the top of a green ridge and the region of Rathcroghan, otherwise Cruachan, which was the royal seat of the kings of Connaught, to say nothing of their queens. The redoubtable Maeve held court here and planned her raid upon the men of Ulster. A mound stands to the south of the crossroads and may or may not be artificial. It has been suggested that it covers a passage grave which would have pre-dated the Iron Age earthworks which are spread all over the ground. There is a standing stone in the centre of a ring fort and then to the south the Cave of Cruachu, one of the better-known entrances to the Underworld. The entrance to the cave is lined with stones, the lintels have ogham inscriptions. The royal seat, like that of Tara, is not on a particularly high hill, but it does command a view over a sizeable piece of country.

At the bottom of the hill, to the southeast, is the village of Tulsk. A mote-and-bailey testify to Anglo-Norman settlement. The mote is topped by the remains of a castle and the village also has the remnants of a Dominican friary of the fifteenth century. The region is a strange one, undoubtedly it went through affluent times but its present state bears few traces of them. This becomes even more striking at the next village, Elphin, which gives its name to a former diocese founded by St Patrick himself. Augustinians and Franciscans had important houses there in the Middle Ages but scarcely a trace remains. The little Church of Ireland church in its time had the dignity of being a cathedral.

From Elphin a road leads northeast to Drumsna and Jamestown, lovely stopping places on a bend of the Shannon.

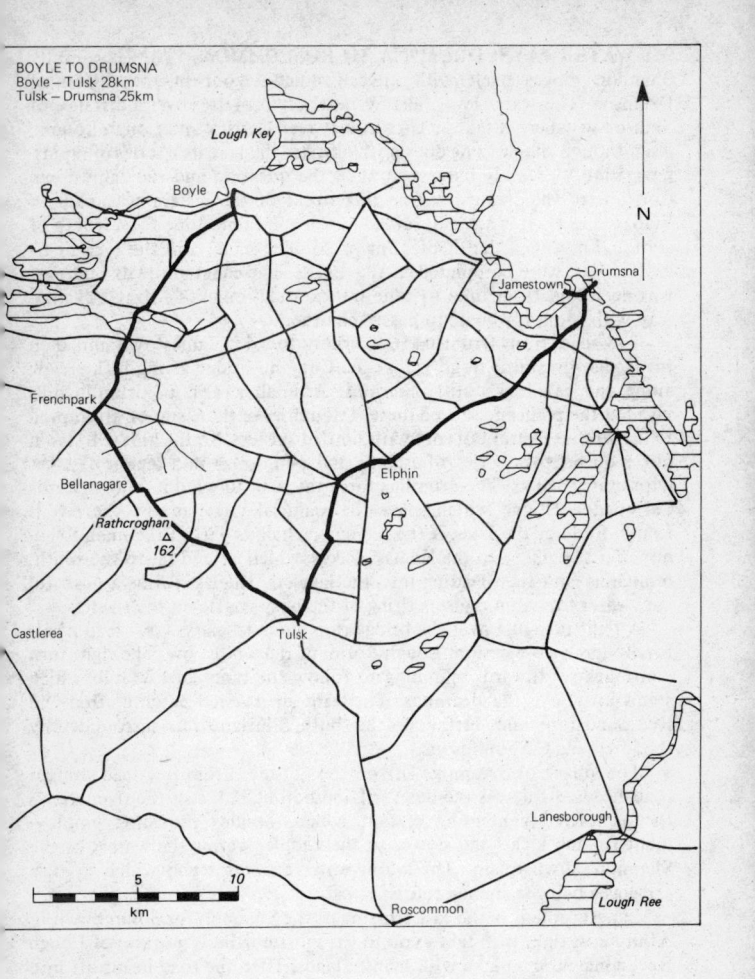

BOYLE TO DRUMSNA
Boyle – Tulsk 28km
Tulsk – Drumsna 25km

35. WATERWAYS: DRUMSNA TO ROSCOMMON

The lazy, lordly Shannon moves itself with unaccustomed vigour in the region of Drumsna. The water level falls by nearly two metres over a distance of 5km or so where it takes a U–turn between Carrick and Lough Boderg. Even though the descent does nothing more than create a series of rapids, navigation by stately barges is out of the question and the Jamestown Cut, one of the greatest engineering works on the system, was made to by-pass the U. It is a canal, carved out of solid limestone for a length of about 2km and a depth of 15m or so. The canal and the lock at its eastern end were completed in the 1770s. The canal in the distant past was neglected from time to time but nowadays makes a straight waterway with room for boats to pass each other.

The road from Drumsna runs briefly towards Jamestown and then turns sharply south to go across the Cut, the bridge giving a fine view along the canal in both directions. A small swarm of drumlin hills invaded the plain and settled there. Tributaries of the Shannon attempted to drown the swarm but met with limited success. So the hills still stand, but reduced to a series of islands and peninsulas in a region of lakes with grassy banks. The drumlins force the road to wind its way towards Carranadoe Bridge which spans the main lake system. To the left is Lough Boderg, the lake of the red cow, which is part of the main Shannon. To the right are the Kilglass Lakes, which extend far to the south, branching and then leading into the lakelets. Kilglass forms a peaceful backwater for cabin cruisers tiring of the busy traffic on the river.

A right turn just over the bridge runs along Kilglass, a left turn heads for Boderg's companion, Lough Bofin, of the white cow. The right turn continues southwards, climbing to follow the range of low hills which stand up above the drumlins. They are an isolated patch of first Old Red Sandstone and, further to the south, Silurian strata surrounded by the low-lying Carboniferous.

The village of Scramoge sits on the hillside. From it a dead straight road heads off across the bog for Lanesborough. Across the river stands the peat-fired generating station which, besides providing employment for the locals and power to the people, warms the waters of the Shannon downstream. The warm water attracts tench which in turn serve as a bait for angling tourists.

Lanesborough is the last crossing of the Shannon for 30km down to Athlone. A right turn takes you to the most northerly portion of Lough Ree, a magnificent lake with many islands. Then the road heads off into the bog again in a straight line all the way to Roscommon town.

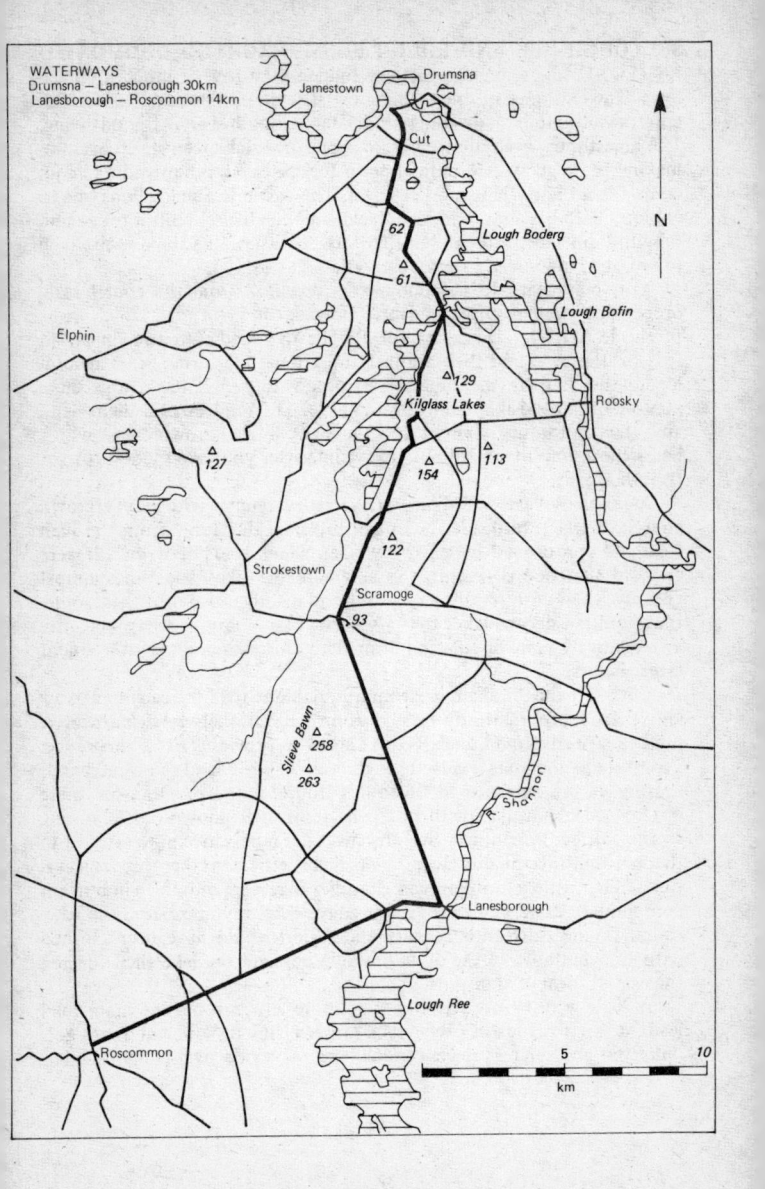

WATERWAYS
Drumsna – Lanesborough 30km
Lanesborough – Roscommon 14km

36. LOUGH REE AND LOUGH FUNSHINAGH: ROSCOMMON TO ATHLONE

Roscommon castle is hidden by a row of modern bungalows. The existence of one of the most affluent castles side by side with comfortable modern dwellings indicates a long history of good living. The limestone gravels are well drained and give rich green sheep pasture, making the place worth defending in the past and still providing an income for an important market town. The castle is a marvellous one to explore, with bastions, barbican, bawn and much else, built, broken and rebuilt from the thirteenth to fifteenth centuries. In a town with much to see, the Dominican Friary deserves a visit too.

You may leave Roscommon by a downhill from the courthouse, proceeding straight on instead of following the main road which bears to the left. After zig-zagging for a while this road runs straight ahead first on the level and then abruptly up a long hill, surmounted according to the map by the ruins of an observatory. Whatever ruins there may be are not visible from the roadside. The road takes a slight bend and then continues straight for the next hill, Carrowmoney, which bears the stump of a windmill, just visible after you take the left turn at the crossroads.

After the village of Rahara, an overgrown hamlet with an overgrown church, a left turn heads for Lough Funshinagh, visible from the high road and approached by a narrow track which leads between ash trees and old thatched cottages. It is a remarkable lake: sometimes almost entirely a fen with hardly any water and mainly a bed of rushes; sometimes quite a decent lake. It is a wildfowl sanctuary and has a healthy and relatively tame population of mallard duck and coots with frequent rarer visitors.

Turn left on the main Roscommon-Athlone road to reach Lecarrow and then sharp right towards St John's Bay, otherwise Rindown. A little canal leads from Lough Ree to Lecarrow, providing a safe anchorage. From there the road leads through well-wooded lands until it bends sharply at the entrance to St John's House. A track leads from there out to the peninsula where stand the ruins of Rindown Castle, dating to the thirteenth century. St John owes his appearance in the region to the fact that the Knights Hospitallers had a settlement there in mediaeval times. The castle and the ruined churches together point to an important community. Road and railway nowadays take wayfarers from the lakeshore. In the thirteenth century the region would have been clothed with impenetrable forest or impassable bog and the lake then formed the easiest form of transport.

A little way before Athlone, one more left turn off the main road leads down to Hodson's Bay. It is rather civilised, with hotel and golf links, but gives an easy access to the lake and a view over many islands.

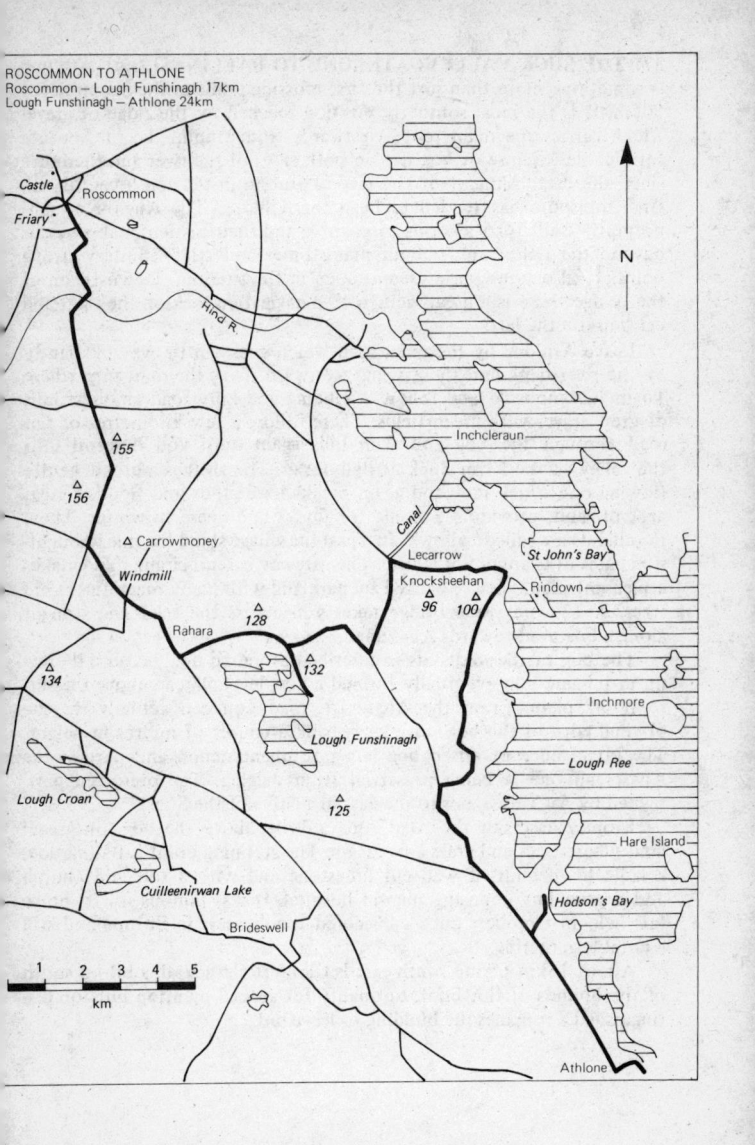

ROSCOMMON TO ATHLONE
Roscommon – Lough Funshinagh 17km
Lough Funshinagh – Athlone 24km

37. THE SUCK VALLEY: ATHLONE TO BALLINASLOE

Athlone is something more than just the first crossing point of the Shannon for 50km. It is the most southerly position reached by the ridge of gravel which carries the main route westwards from Dublin. To the south a formidable expanse of bog lies on both sides of the river and therefore since the establishment of the city of Dublin in the tenth century all land transport has tended to head for Athlone. The Anglo-Normans promptly built fortifications to guard it and their castle remains to this day on the right bank, rebuilt many times and still a military strong point. It also houses a museum, open in the summer. Downstream of the bridge there is a great weir, with a navigation lock on the right and eel traps on the left.

Leave Athlone by the main road which goes a little way pleasantly by the river bank and then swings westward. Take the right turn where Tuam is signposted and follow a winding and hilly road amongst hills of grey gravel with green fields. There follow a few kilometres of flat road through the bog and then hills again until you descend into the valley of the River Suck at Ballyforan. The river is a broad, gently flowing one which now and again breaks its bounds and floods a great area of land, providing a home for ducks and geese in winter. These floodlands are called 'callows'. Just past the village stand the fine wrought-iron gates of Claremount House. The gateway is semi-circular and makes a pleasant picnic place, backed by parkland with many magnificent old trees. A 13-eyed stone bridge takes you across the river and straight along a bog road towards Ahascragh.

The bog of the midlands is described as 'raised bog' because it grew up in fenland and eventually formed a low, level plateau above the surrounding plain. From the Ahascragh road you can actually see the original edge of the bog, forming a bank a couple of metres in height. The intact edge of raised bog is a rare phenomenon and part of the Ahascragh one is being preserved from digging. The preserved part, owned by An Taisce, lies to the east in a curve of the Suck.

From Ahascragh the road runs a little above the bog, on gravel land where trees and grass grow again. The stopping point is Ballinasloe, a large town built of well cut limestone and with a splendid church and a grim but imposing mental hospital. It was famous for its horse fair held in October, once considered the greatest in Europe and still a notable gathering.

About 15km to the south-east is Clonfert Cathedral, a bit far south of the bounds of this book to qualify for special mention but too distinguished a romanesque building to leave out.

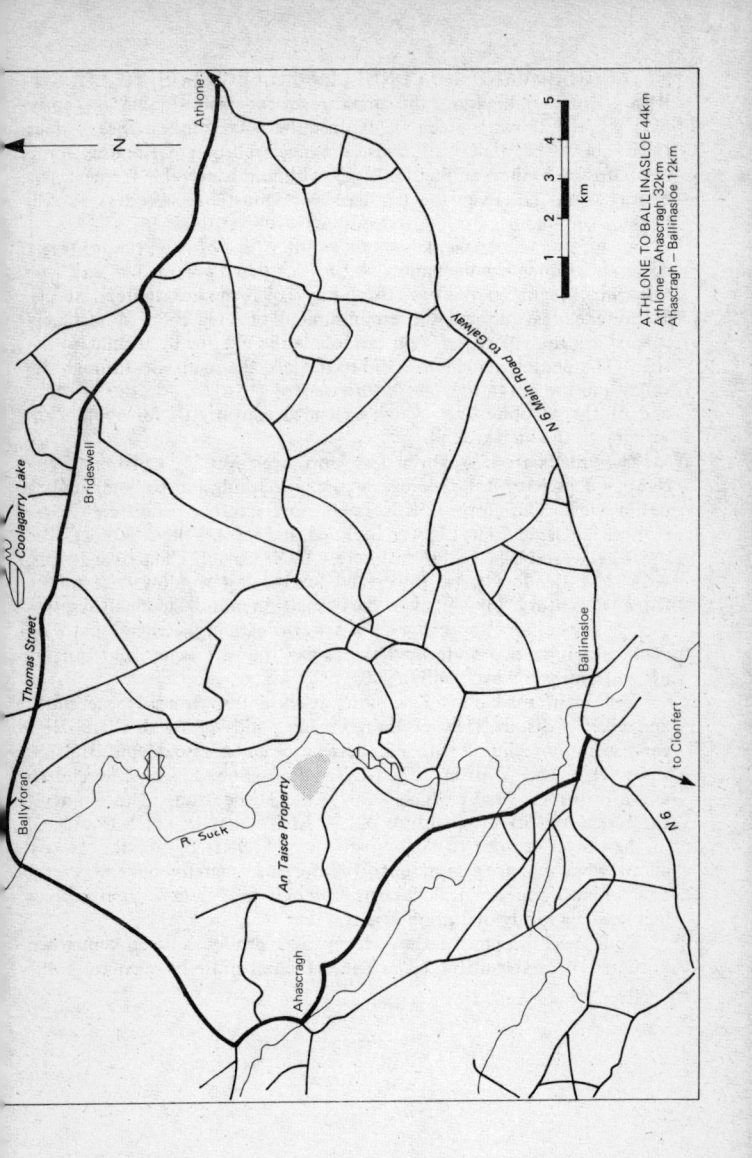

ATHLONE TO BALLINASLOE 44km
Athlone – Ahascragh 32km
Ahascragh – Ballinasloe 12km

38. AUGHRIM AND KILCONNELL: BALLINASLOE TO LOUGHREA

From Ballinasloe the main road for Galway climbs gently over gravel hills with green fields on either side. Lines of beech trees tower above the stone walls and there may well be great houses in the area. However, they are hidden away within impenetrable fastnesses of exotic woodland. Even the familiar beech must be classed as exotic, having been imported in the sixteenth or seventeenth century.

A narrow church steeple announces the village of Aughrim, of tragic or treasured memory depending on the foot you dig with. The Battle of Aughrim, fought on the twelfth of July 1691, marked the end of the Jacobite endeavour and the establishment of King Billy. A fast new road skirts the village, but you can follow the old one by turning to the right. The church stands on a hill to the left, the road runs through the valley and the hill to the right, with a trace of a castle, marks the northern end of the Jacobite lines which extended southwards for about 2km keeping to the high ground.

Two roads from Aughrim lead north-westerly for Kilconnell: the righthand one runs at the edge of the gravel hills and so commands a better view. The glory of Kilconnell, now a rather forgotten village, is the Franciscan friary. It was founded in 1353 on the site of a Celtic monastery established 800 years before by St Conall. The existing ruins, with their slender square tower and lovely west window date to the fifteenth century. Like many of the Franciscan ruins, Kilconnell deserves a close inspection. You can get a key to the gate in the village and then walk to admire two sculptured tombs and the very extensive remnants of the friary's domestic buildings.

The main road after Kilconnell takes a turn towards the south and gives a distant view of the grim, grey hills of north Clare. New Inn has a funny church with a modern porch and a little steeple. Bullaun, the next village is distinguished by a pink school and a white church and a turn to the right which leads to the Turoe Stone. This is one of the rare survivors of sculpture of the La Tene style which flourished in the centuries prior to the Christian era. Archaeology books are coy about what the stone represents. Ill-informed amateurs have no doubt concerning its anatomical import. It stands in a field with fine trees just beside a lovely old farmhouse.

Loughrea, the end of the journey, is a proud and well-kept town bordered by a beautiful lake. The cathedral must be seen from the inside.

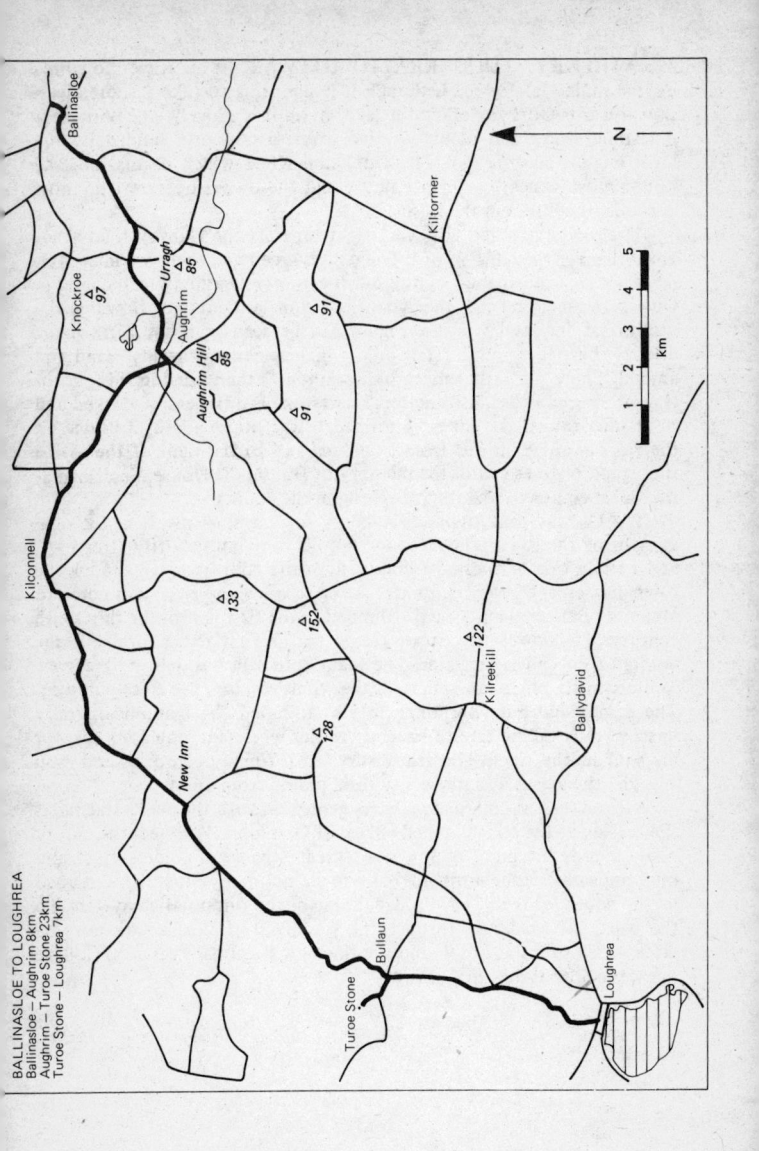

BALLINASLOE TO LOUGHREA
Ballinasloe – Aughrim 8km
Aughrim – Turoe Stone 23km
Turoe Stone – Loughrea 7km

39. ATHENRY: LOUGHREA TO GALWAY You leave Loughrea by the main Galway road, though it is tempting to take a short diversion towards Gort to follow the lake shore: it is a lovely lake with clear limestone water and plenty of fine trout, assiduously tended by the local angling association. The Dunkellin River which drains the lake runs almost beneath a private house and the owner operates the most convenient eel trap in the business.

At a neat, thatched cottage a right turn off the Galway road heads for Athenry, the King's Ford. The land is green and there are many fine trees, often wind-shaped by the south-westerly weather which comes in with little shelter from the Atlantic. From late summer onwards the traditional haystacks of the region can be seen: the hay after being dried is heaped around a tall pole which anchors it against wind and animal. There are rather more old farmhouses than usual in this part of Galway, perhaps because the local limestone is quite easily worked and built into robust dwellings. A ruined tower house guards a bridge on the river about 8km out from Loughrea and to the right of the road a fine stand of trees guards the memory of Dunsandle House, described as the finest eighteenth-century dwelling in the county.

The Galway road bypasses Athenry so you must divert to the right in sight of the town. The great town walls were built shortly after 1312 and remain one of the most complete in the country, even though the town has escaped their embrace. After crossing the river you come to Meiler de Bermingham's castle founded in the first half of the thirteenth century. The lower two storeys date to the first foundation but the pointed roof gables are later. The main door still has delicately carved capitals to its pillars and many of the windows also have fine sculpture. The same Meiler de Bermingham also founded the Dominican friary nearby, thus taking care of his body in this world and doing his best for his soul in the next. The friary survived for many centuries and even enjoyed the status of a university for a period from 1644.

After Athenry, the road wanders gently through the plains and meets the seaside at the still-thatched village of Oranmore. A sixteenth-century castle guards the inlet. At low tide a great expanse of golden wrack and mud appears: rather surprisingly there are not many birds there. A road to the south leads to Clarinbridge, home of the finest native oysters. To the west, the road runs through the woodland of Merlin Park hospital after which suburbs, hotels and the fine new Regional Technical College mark the approaches to Galway.

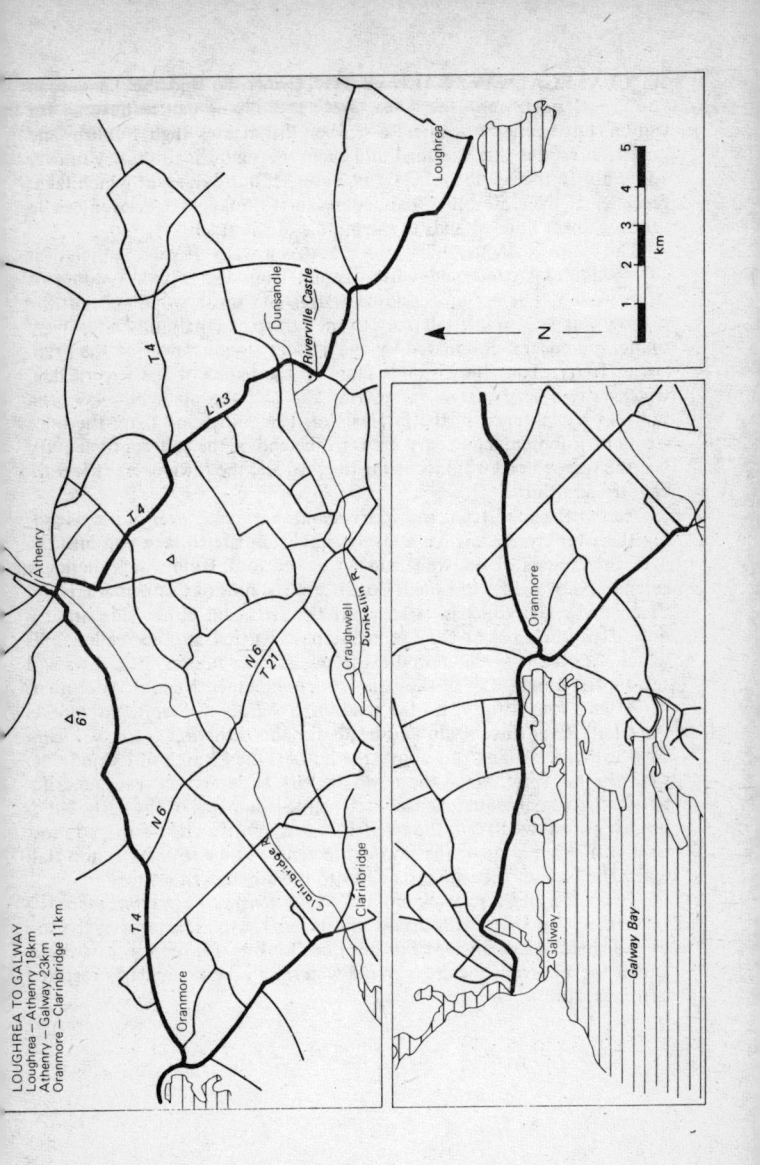

LOUGHREA TO GALWAY
Loughrea – Athenry 18km
Athenry – Galway 23km
Oranmore – Clarinbridge 11km

40. CLAREGALWAY: GALWAY TO TUAM

To find the Tuam road you travel northwards past the Galway shopping centre heading for Dublin, but turning off where a signboard indicates Sligo. Suburbs and industrial estates line the road and there is a signpost to show you over a low hill to the celebrated Galway Races, a four-day event which takes precedence over all other happenings in Connaught. A seventeenth-century tower house stands in the middle of the track.

The route is slightly hilly, going between walls of stone, much of it cut or quarried stone and quite distinct from the rounded stones of Roscommon. There are occasional hedges and scrub woodland but the shallow soil discourages tall trees. From the top of a little hill Claregalway suddenly appears, dominated by the slender square tower of the Franciscan friary. The friary stands close to the banks of the River Clare, which was a lazy stream wandering through the plain but has been savagely straightened in the interests of reclaiming land from the once frequent flooding. The friary dates to the end of the thirteenth century but the splayed east window facing the road and the tower were fifteenth-century additions.

Across the road from the friary stands a square tower house, guarding the river crossing. It has a lovely spiral staircase to take you into the dark thicknesses of the walls and up to the roof, from which there is a splendid view across to Lough Corrib and the hills of Connemara. From Claregalway the going is rather flat, the fields on either side are dry nowadays but most of the life in the past centred around the low hills which stood above the periodical floods. Tower houses, ring forts and substantial farmhouses of the eighteenth or nineteenth centuries abound.

After a long straight bit the road turns sharply at Claretuam, crosses the Clare River once again and heads for the cathedral town of Tuam. Two cathedrals stand out above the houses: the Church of Ireland one, with the tall spire, being the more ancient. It deserves a visit especially to see the romanesque chancel arch: all that remains of the early building which survived from the twelfth century until a fire destroyed most of it in 1767. Fabric of the fourteenth century now forms a Synod Hall while the bulk of the cathedral dates to the nineteenth century.

Tuam is a place to walk around. In the centre of the town there is a very fine cross shaft with lovely interlacing beasts. The cross at the top of the shaft is also ancient but does not look as if it belongs just there. Down the hill from the cross an old watermill is being tenderly restored as a museum.

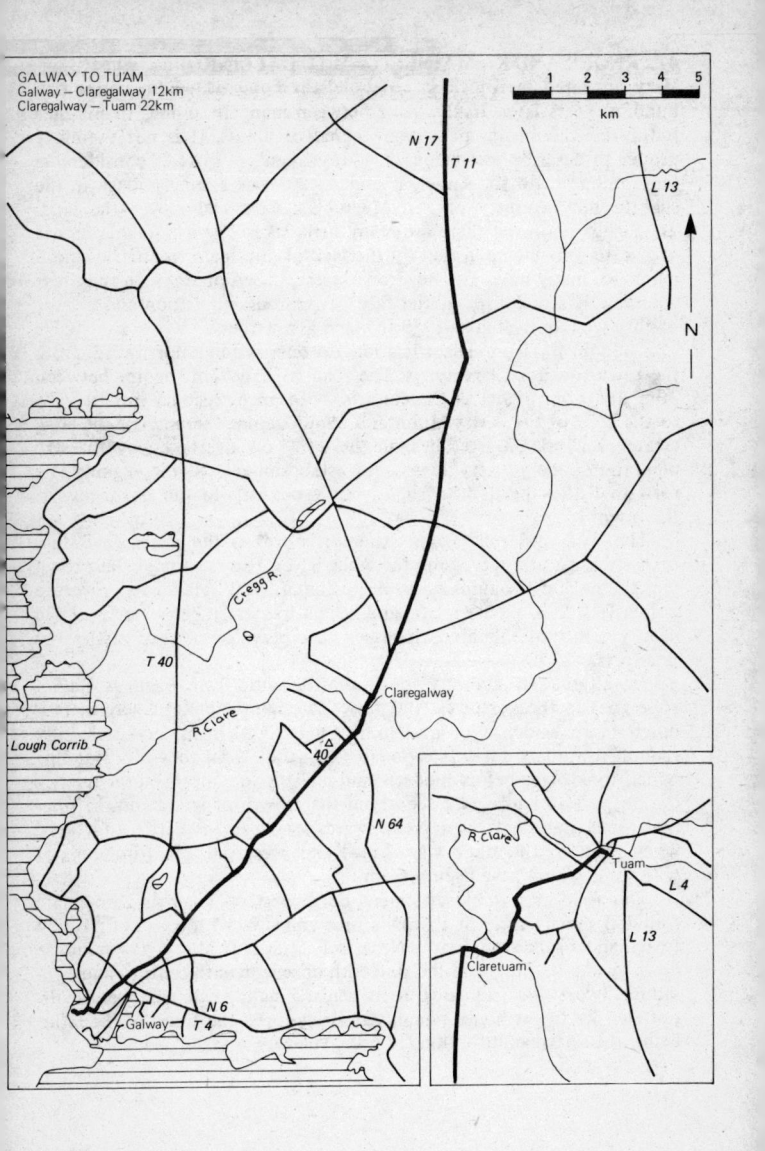

GALWAY TO TUAM
Galway – Claregalway 12km
Claregalway – Tuam 22km

41. KNOCK AND KILMAINE: TUAM TO BALLINROBE

The Virgin Mary appeared in Knock in 1879 and the Pope visited the shrine one hundred years later. In the years between many thousands of pilgrims journeyed there and many were cured of illness. It is not therefore proper to describe the region as 'godforsaken', in spite of considerable temptation to do so. Knock is and always was a small village in the slightly hilly country of east Mayo. Glacial gravels cover the land, drainage is poor and there are many little lakes The intractable nature of the region is emphasised by the lack of any major monastic settlements for many miles around. Nonetheless, the vision was seen and those who saw it stood firm in the face of rigorous inquisition and a great basilica was completed in 1979 to stand as a witness.

The journey from Tuam is a longish one, heading northwards from the town towards Claremorris. The road is fairly flat, keeping between 30m and 60m as far as Claremorris, with an occasional distant view to the west of the Partry Mountains. Approaching Claremorris the large estate of Castlemagarret lies on the left, now overtaken by forestry plantation, one of very few major establishments in the region. The road to Knock heads into slightly hilly country to the north-east of the town.

The westward road from Claremorris crosses the plains to Ballinrobe, crossing and recrossing the Robe River. It was an important town in its time and the ruins of an Augustinian friary remain to prove the point. It still is a busy place and seems to have taken over from the nearby centre of Kilmaine which lies surrounded by ruins of castles and ring-forts.

An alternative and very much shorter route from Tuam to Ballinrobe goes to the northwest and passes through the plains where there is much more evidence of past human activity than in the bleak hilly ground towards Knock. It is possible that the extensive winter flooding which took place before modern land reclamation improved the quality of the pasture land and discouraged the growth of woodland. In summer there would have been green swards for sheep and cattle. In winter, when most of the stock were killed and preserved, great numbers of wild geese would have been present.

The first important settlement north-west of Tuam is Kilbennan, founded shortly after St Patrick's time and now with traces of a round tower and Franciscan friary. Next is Feartagar Castle, a tower house built by the de Burgos in the sixteenth or seventeenth century and containing two spiral staircases in its walls. Finally, Kilmaine stands surrounded by tower house remains and ring-forts, the finest of the latter being at Lisnatreanduff, 2km from the village.

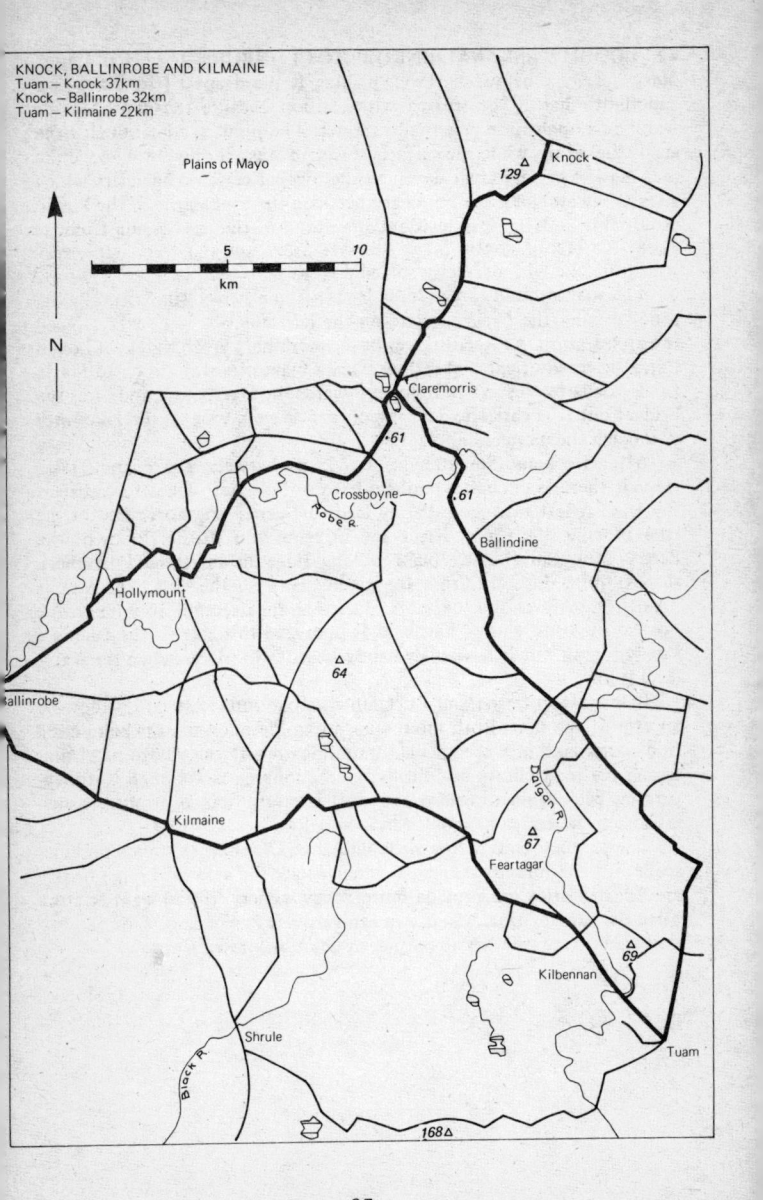

KNOCK, BALLINROBE AND KILMAINE
Tuam – Knock 37km
Knock – Ballinrobe 32km
Tuam – Kilmaine 22km

42. LOUGH MASK: BALLINROBE TO CLONBUR

The bed of Lough Mask lies 39m below sea level, making it the deepest Irish lake. This superlative has to be treated with caution because the depth of the water in Lough Erne is actually greater. The point is that Lough Erne starts higher up while the surface of Lough Mask is only 18m above the sea. Mask owes its great depth to the digging action of glaciers which scoured away along the boundary between the tough grits of the Partry Mountains and the less resistant limestone of the east. Aside from its claim for record depth, Mask deserves attention as a very large, very beautiful lake with perfectly splendid trout.

The road around Lough Mask leads off in a straight line from Ballinrobe, passing the Creagh estate on the left which now houses a sheep research station. At Keel Bridge the extraordinary green waters of Lough Carra lie to the right and a slow stream makes its way down to Mask. Little roads to the left lead down towards the lake before and after the bridge; but it is easier to journey on and leave a visit to the lake until you reach the western shore.

After Keel another straight road runs between Carra and Mask, though there is enough woodland here to hide both lakes for most of the way. A left turn from Partry leads off across the north end of the lake crossing the Cloon River and bringing you to the slopes of the Partry Mountains. They make a long ridge of boggy and heathery slopes, quite different from the green plains to the east. The rock is mainly Ordovician and therefore older than the Carboniferous limestone on the opposite shore. The land is poor and this side of the lake is a lonely region but it has lovely sandy beaches in places when the water level is low.

Below Maumtrasna and Buckaun the road runs westward, following an arm of the lake. Both mountains are noble ones and Buckaun has a fine corrie lake in a spectacular amphitheatre. At the village of Maumtrasna the road climbs and heads for the long narrow Lough Nafooey, turning back again to follow the most westerly branch of Mask which is narrow enough to be crossed by a bridge.

The journey ends at the little village of Clonbur. It stands on limestone but the hills to the south which block the view of Lough Corrib are Silurian grits and provide more boggy scenery. If you want to complete the Lough Mask circuit you can turn left 2km east of Clonbur, but that part of the lake has already been described under Cong.

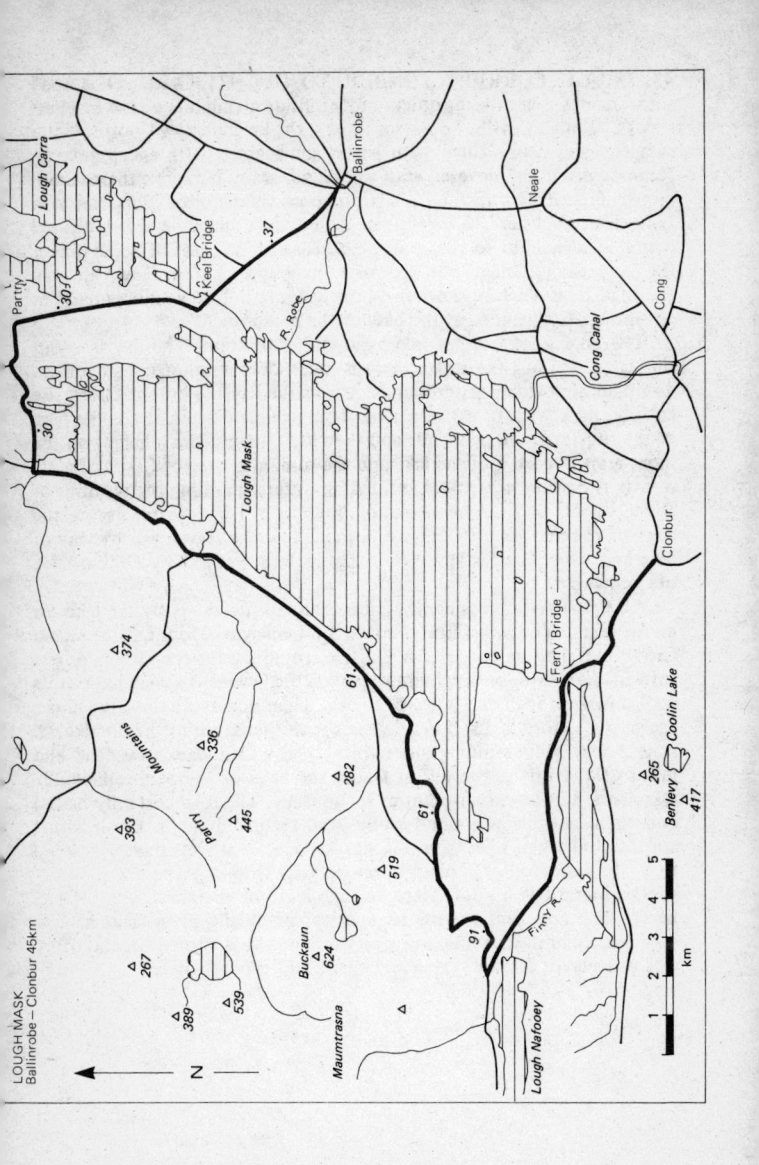

LOUGH MASK
Ballinrobe – Clonbur 45km

43. LOUGH CORRIB: CLONBUR TO OUGHTERARD

The road south from Clonbur leads quickly to a hillside giving one of the loveliest views of Lough Corrib. To the south-west the long, narrow Dooros peninsula encloses a bay filled with islets: some green with sheep grazing, some deserted and covered with woodland. Many birds live there. Common gulls, tufted duck and mallard choose the wooded islets; flat low-lying ones such as Cleenillaun are tenanted by black-headed gulls and common terns. Far to the south, clothed with a forest of Scots pine is the holy island, Inchagoill with its romanesque church. Down the hill the road hugs the lake shore for some distance before heading inland to go through Cornamona at the base of the peninsula.

The lake on the other side looks quite different. The bay is about the same size but the water there is much deeper, plunging steeply to 46m and almost free from islands. Across the bay the hills of Glann rise steeply, dark with forest in places. You go inland again across the base of the shorter Doon peninsula and then look down from a height on the most remote corner of the lake and the romantic keep of Castlekirk. Its setting is perfect, a sentinel in the dark waters, guarding the pastures of Joyce's River and the fastnesses of the hills of Connemara. Before the days of rail and road the easiest approach to the region was by way of lake and river. The castle was a royal one, built in 1235 by Fedlim King of Connaught.

After the river crossing at Maum there are no roads by the lake for many miles. You must travel south by Leckavrea Mountain to Maam Cross and then eastwards for Oughterard to regain the shore. A left turn in the centre of Oughterard crosses the Owenriff which has cut its way down through the limestone rock. Then you reach the lake shore again, once more in a region of islands with Inchagoill to the north-east. It is a very hilly, winding and narrow road which leads to a dead end just to the south of the hill of Doon, the head of the peninsula which was crossed at an earlier point of the journey. The road certainly has an end there and it has a wonderfully dead feeling about it. Doon is just another hill when seen from the north but here it rises dark and steep from the water's edge, a place of mystery far from anywhere.

Oughterard is a good place to take leave of the north-west. It is a lively shopping centre with its eyes set on fertile plains and a busy lake which brings people and profits. Its back is turned on the other side of Ireland: remote, harsh and beautiful beyond belief.

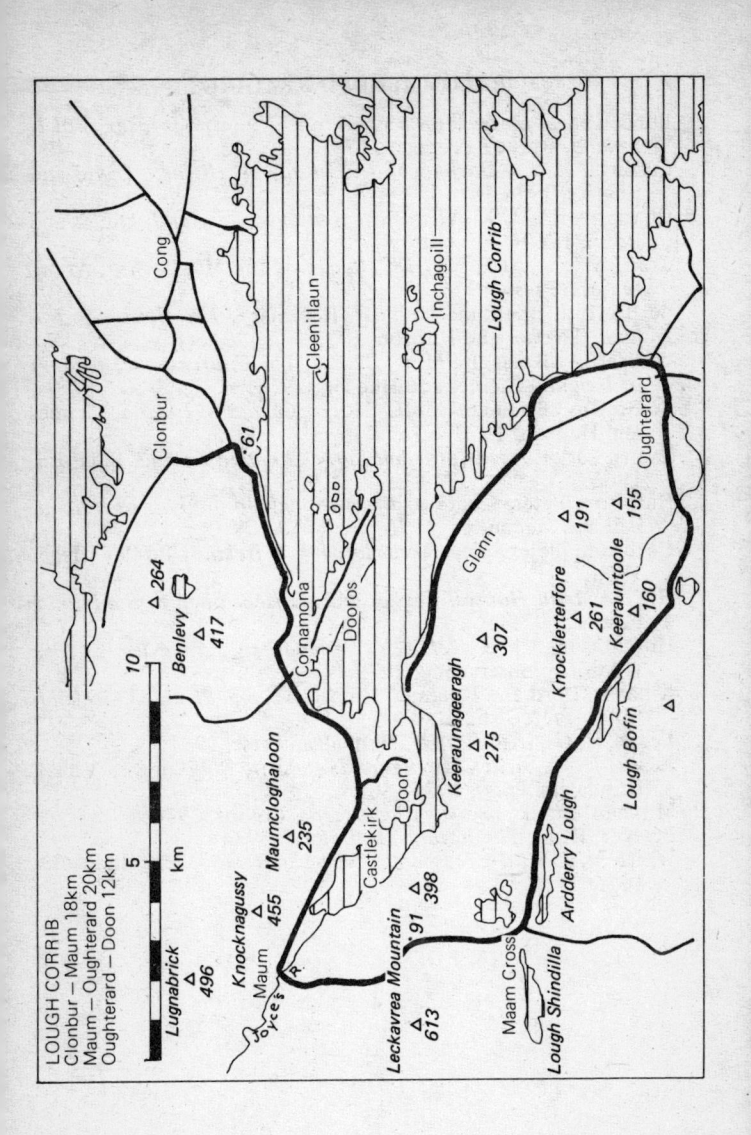

LOUGH CORRIB
Clonbur – Maum 18km
Maum – Oughterard 20km
Oughterard – Doon 12km

RECOMMENDED READING

Bence-Jones, Mark, *Burke's Guide to Country Houses, Vol.1, Ireland*, Burke's Peerage, 1978.

Casserly, H. C., *Outline of Irish Railway History*, David and Charles, 1974.

Charlesworth, J. K., *Historical Geology of Ireland*, Oliver and Boyd, 1963.

Craig, Maurice, *Classic Irish Houses of the Middle Size*, Architectural Press, 1976.

de Breffny, Brian and ffolliott, Rosemary, *The Houses of Ireland*, Thames and Hudson, 1975.

de Breffny, Brian and Mott, George, *The Churches and Abbeys of Ireland*, Thames and Hudson, 1976.

de Breffny, Brian and Mott, George, *Castles of Ireland*, Thames and Hudson, 1977.

Evans, Estyn, *Prehistoric and Early Christian Ireland*, Batsford, 1966.

Harbison, Peter, *Guide to the National Monuments of Ireland*, Gill and Macmillan, 1975.

Harbison, Peter, *The Archaeology of Ireland*, Bodley Head, 1976.

HITHA, *Irish Houses, Castles and Gardens open to the Public*, Easons, 1979.

Hutchinson, Clive, *Ireland's Wetlands and their Birds*, Irish Wildbird Conservancy, 1979.

Killanin, Lord and Duignan, Michael V., *Shell Guide to Ireland*, Ebury Press 1962.

Leask, H. G., *Irish Castles*, Dundalgan Press, 1951.

Leask, H. G., *Irish Churches and Monastic Buildings*, (3 Vols.), Dundalgan Press, 1955–60.

Mitchell, Frank, *The Irish Landscape*, Collins, 1976.

Praeger, R. L., *The Botanist in Ireland*, 1934.

Whittow, J. B., *Geology and Scenery in Ireland*, Penguin Books, 1975.

INDEX
(to route numbers)

Aasleagh Falls	10	Benbulbin	19
Achill	12	Bengorm	10
Agraffard, Lough	2	Bertraghboy	5
Ahascragh	37	Big Isle	26
Alcock and Brown	4	Black Pig's Race	31
Allen, Lough	31	Blacksod Bay	13
Anure, Lough	23	Blanket bog	13
Aran Islands	6	Bloody Foreland	23
Aranmore	22	Blue Stack Mountains	29
Arbutus	18	Bofin, Lough	2
Ardara	22	Boyle	33
Ards Peninsula	24, 25	Boyle River	32
Arrow, Lough	33	Bricklieve Mountains	33
Ashford Castle	8	Broadhaven	13
Aspen	9	Bruckless	20
Athenry	39	Buckaun	42
Athlone	37	Bundoran	19
Aughnanure Castle	1	Bunnaton	25
Aughrim	38	Burnthouse	1
Aughrus More	4	Burrishoole	11
		Burt	26
Ball Hill	29	Burtonport	22
Ballina	14, 16		
Ballinakill Harbour	3	Calabber River	24
Ballinasloe	37	Carna	5
Ballinrobe	9, 41	Carndonagh	27
Ballintober	9	Carolan	32
Ballybofey	29	Carra, Lough	9
Ballycastle	14	Carrick	21
Ballyconneely	4	Carrowkeel	28
Ballyfarnan	32	Carrowkilleen	15
Ballyglass	14	Carrowmore	17
Ballymote	33	Carrowmore Lake	13
Ballynahinch	5	Cashel	5
Ballysadare	16	Casla	6
Ballyshannon	19, 20	Castlebar	9
Bangor Erris	13	Castle Firbis	16
Barnacle geese	19	Castlekirk	43
Barnesmore Gap	29	Clare, River	7
Basking sharks	12	Clare Island	10
Beagh, Lough	24	Claremorris	41
Belderg	14	Clarinbridge	39
Belleek	30	Cleggan	3, 4
Belmullet	13	Clew Bay	10

93

Clifden	4	Dunlewey	24
Clonbur	42		
Clonfert	37	Easky	16
Cong	8, 9	Elphin	34
Conn, Lough	15	Erne, Lough	30
Connemara marble	1	Errew	15
Corraun	13	Erriff, River	10
Corrib	1, 7, 43	Errigal	24
Corrigeenroe	32	Errisbeg	4
Costelloe	6	Eske, Lough	29
Creeslough	25	Eske, River	20
Creevelea Friary	18		
Creggan Lough	10	Fahan	26
Cregg River	7	Feartagar	41
Croaghaun	12	Fee, Lough	3
Croagh Patrick	11	Feeagh, Lough	11
Crockalough	27	Finn River	29
Crohy Head	22	Foraminifera	4
Cuchullain	17	Fossils	19
Cullin, Lough	15	Foyle, Lough	28
Curlew Mountains	33	Frenchpark	34
Currane Youth Hostel	13	Funshinagh, Lough	36
		Furnace, Lough	11
Deerpark	18		
Delphi	10	Galway	1, 6, 7
Derg, Lough	30	Gara, Lough	33
Derryclare	5	Garavogue River	18
Devilsmother	10	Gill, Lough	18
Diarmuid and Grainne	22	Glenamoy	14
Doe Castle	25	Glencar	18
Dog's Bay	4	Glencolumbkille	21
Donegal Castle	20	Glencullin Lough	10
Donegal Friary	20	Glenfarne	31
Doogort	12	Glengad Head	27
Doo Lough	10	Glenveagh Castle	24
Doon	43	Gortahork	23
Dooncarton	14	Gortmore	6
Doon Castle	4	Grange	19
Dowra	31	Granuaile	5
Dromahair	18	Greencastle	28
Drowes, River	19	Grianan of Aileach	28
Drumcliff	19		
Drumsna	35	Headford	7, 8
Dunfanaghy	23, 25	Hodson's Bay	36
Dunglow	22	Horn Head	25
Dunkellin River	39		
Dunkineely	20	Iar-connaught	5

Inch	26	Letterkenny	26, 28
Inishbofin	3	Lissadell	19
Inishcrone	16	Lithothamnion	5
Inishmacatreer	8	Loughrea	38
Inishmaine	8	Louisburgh	10
Inishowen	27		
Inishtrahull	27	Maam Cross	2
Innisfree	18	Macnean, Lough	31
		Maeve, Queen	17
Jamestown	35	Magilligan	28
		Malin Head	27
Keadew	32	Malinmore	21
Keel	12	Mallaranny	12
Keem	12	Mallard	9
Keshcorran	33	Mannin Bay	4
Key, Lough	32	Manorcunningham	26
Kilbennan	41	Manorhamilton	18, 30
Kilcar	21	Mask, Lough	8, 42
Kilclooney	22	Maumtrasna	10, 42
Kilconnell	38	Maumturk Mountains	2
Kilglass Lakes	35	McSwyne's Castle	20
Kilkieran	5, 6	Mediterranean heather	3, 12
Killala	14	Meelagh, Lough	32
Killala Bay	16	Megalithic tombs	17, 32
Killary	10	Menlough	7
Killary Harbour	2	Moher Lough	10
Kilmaine	41	Moore Hall	9
Kilronan	32	Mountcharles	20
Killybegs	20	Mourne, Lough	29
Killydonnell	26	Moville	28
King's Mountain	18, 19	Moy, River	15
Knappagh	10	Moycullen	1
Knock	41	Moygarra Castle	33
Knockalla	25	Moyne	14
Knocknahar	17	Moytirra	32
Knocknarea	17	Moytura	8
Knockvicar	32	Muckish	24
Kylemore	3	Mulrany	12
		Mulroy Bay	25
Lahanagh	18	Murrisk	11
Lanesborough	35	Mweenish	5
Lecan	16		
Lecarrow	36	Nafooey, Lough	42
Leckavrea Mountain	2	Nephin	15
Leenaun	2	Nephinbeg	11
Lennan, River	26	Newport	11
Letterfrack	3	Newtowncunningham	25

O'Donnell	29	St Brendan	7
Omey Island	4	St Dabeoc's heath	3
Oranmore	39	St John's Bay	36
Oughterard	2, 43	St Lasair	32
Owenriff, River	2	St Mura	25
Owenwee, River	10	Salmon Research Trust	11
Ox Mountains	16, 18, 19	Screeb	6
		Shannon, River	35
Parke's Castle	18	Sheefry Hills	10
Partry Mountains	42	Sheep Haven	25
Pearse, P. H.	6	Shoveler	9
Pettigoe	30	Skean, Lough	32
Poisoned Glen	24	Slieve Anierin	31
Pollacappul Lough	3	Slieve League	21
Pollatomish	14	Slievemore	12
Pontoon	15	Slieve Snaght	27
Portsalon	25	Sligo	19
Poulacappal Lough	3	Slish Wood	18
Pullans	20	Strandhill	17
		Stranorlar	29
		Streamstown Bay	4
Raised bog	37	Streedagh	19
Rathcroghan	34	Suck, River	37
Rathfran	14	Swilly, Lough	25, 26
Rathmelton	25, 26		
Rathmullan	25	Termon Point	13
Ray	23	Toombeola	5
Ree, Lough	35, 36	Tory Island	23
Rindown	36	Trá na Rossan	25
Rockfleet	12	Tullaghan	19
Rockingham	32	Tulsk	34
Roscommon	36	Turoe Stone	38
Rosserk	14	Twelve Pins	3, 5
Ross Errilly	8		
Rosses Point	19	Westport	9, 10, 11
Roundstone	4, 5	Whooper swans	25